Dec 2014

Between Slavery and Freedom

The African American History Series

Series Editors:
Jacqueline M. Moore, Austin College
Nina Mjagkij, Ball State University

Traditionally, history books tend to fall into two categories: books academics write for each other, and books written for popular audiences. Historians often claim that many of the popular authors do not have the proper training to interpret and evaluate the historical evidence. Yet, popular audiences complain that most historical monographs are inaccessible because they are too narrow in scope or lack an engaging style. This series, which will take both chronological and thematic approaches to topics and individuals crucial to an understanding of the African American experience, is an attempt to address that problem. The books in this series, written in lively prose by established scholars, are aimed primarily at nonspecialists. They focus on topics in African American history that have broad significance and place them in their historical context. While presenting sophisticated interpretations based on primary sources and the latest scholarship, the authors tell their stories in a succinct manner, avoiding jargon and obscure language. They include selected documents that allow readers to judge the evidence for themselves and to evaluate the authors' conclusions. Bridging the gap between popular and academic history, these books bring the African American story to life.

Volumes Published

Between Slavery and Freedom

Free People of Color in America From
Settlement to the Civil War

Julie Winch

ROWMAN & LITTLEFIELD PUBLISHERS, INC.
Lanham • Boulder • New York • Toronto • Plymouth, UK

Published by Rowman & Littlefield
4501 Forbes Boulevard, Suite 200, Lanham, Maryland 20706
www.rowman.com

10 Thornbury Road, Plymouth PL6 7PP, United Kingdom

Distributed by National Book Network

British Library Cataloguing in Publication Information Available

Library of Congress Cataloging-in-Publication Data

Winch, Julie, 1953–
Between slavery and freedom : free people of color in America from settlement to the Civil War / Julie Winch.
pages cm. — (The African American history series)
Includes bibliographical references.
ISBN 978-0-7425-5114-5 (cloth : alk. paper) — ISBN 978-0-7425-5115-2 (electronic)
1. Free African Americans—History. 2. Free African Americans—Social conditions. 3. Free African Americans—Attitudes—History. 4. United States—Race relations—History. I. Title.
E185.18.W57 2014
973'.0496073—dc23   2013045609

♾™ The paper used in this publication meets the minimum requirements of American National Standard for Information Sciences—Permanence of Paper for Printed Library Materials, ANSI/NISO Z39.48-1992.

Printed in the United States of America

In memory of Janet Harrison Shannon
A great friend and a ready listener

Contents

List of Tables

Acknowledgments

I cannot begin my list of people to thank without acknowledging Jacqueline Moore and Nina Mjagkij, the tireless and energetic editors of Rowman & Littlefield's African American History series. Jackie and Nina suggested the topic for *Between Slavery and Freedom* and guided me through the process of writing it. They encouraged me every step of the way. When other projects sidetracked me, they understood, but they kept me focused. They took my early efforts, labored over them with an admirable mix of tact and skill, and helped me reshape a series of long and unwieldy drafts into a shorter, tighter narrative. Without their efforts this book would never have seen the light of day.

Jackie and Nina have been wonderful editors, and my acknowledgments fall far short of the debt of gratitude I owe them. Rowman & Littlefield's senior executive editor, Jonathan Sisk, and assistant editor, Benjamin Verdi, have fielded innumerable questions about everything from page length to file downloads and have done so with unfailing patience. I am grateful to them for their guidance and their forbearance.

I have incurred many other debts of gratitude. The students in my graduate and undergraduate classes at the University of Massachusetts Boston (UMB) have shared this journey with me. They have heard about the book project for several years. They have read document selections, chapter outlines, and in some instances, entire chapters. They have offered advice and constructive criticism. Above all, they have posed challenging questions that often made me stop and think. UMB students are perennially inquisitive, and that is what has made teaching at UMB such a joy over the years. What starts out as "This may be a stupid question, but . . ." never is. I offer my heartfelt thanks to all of my students, even those who eventually decided to major in something other than history.

My husband, Louis S. Cohen, has helped in so many ways. He has listened and he has sympathized. He has provided "tech support" and has done battle with my computer on numerous occasions. He has kept the household together and he has given me the time I needed to read, to write, and to reflect. I have dedicated other books to Lou, and I know he does not begrudge the fact that this book is dedicated not to him but to the memory of our mutual friend, Janet Harrison Shannon. Her insightfulness, her enthusiasm, her good humor, and her graciousness are greatly missed but fondly remembered.

INTRODUCTION

~

On Liberty's Borderlands

On the eve of the Civil War, the nation's free black population stood at almost half a million, compared to just under four million slaves. About half of the free people lived in the Northern and Western states that had outlawed slavery, and half in the South where slavery was still legal. But while these numbers are obviously important, they tell only a small part of the story. Census takers missed many rural communities and chose not to enter some poor urban neighborhoods. The census does not tell us how many black people kept out of sight when a white stranger started asking intrusive questions. We do not know how often people who were passing as free lied about their status because they were still technically enslaved, or in how many instances light-skinned "colored persons" ended up in the "whites" column on the census form. Above all, the census cannot tell us how individual free men and women of color lived their lives. One truth that does emerge with undeniable clarity, though, from even a cursory glance at the data, is that freedom was something less than true freedom for black people. Approximately half a million African Americans were not slaves in 1860, but they were not free as whites understood the term. They constituted a segment of American society that defied easy categorization: they were free but at the same time they were not free. Theirs was a marginal status somewhere between slave and citizen.

To dwell in the ill-defined borderlands between bondage and freedom was not a comfortable existence, yet it was the only reality hundreds of thousands of blacks knew. Their white friends and neighbors often failed to appreciate how fraught with danger and disappointment that existence could be. All but a handful of white antislavery radicals thought of slavery and freedom as absolutes. In their eyes, a black man or woman ceased being another person's property and joined the ranks of the free. Their journey was done. But as black people who made that move into freedom tried to explain, it was not that simple.

Slavery and freedom were not polar opposites for black Americans. An individual could be more or less free depending on his or her individual circumstances. The enslaved used their wits to try to make their bondage less onerous. They exploited the situations in which they found themselves, while never relinquishing the hope of one day walking away from slavery entirely. They sought to earn money or amass a few possessions that they could call their own, get time away from their owners to spend with family and friends, learn to read and write when the opportunity arose, and in short to do anything and everything to come closer to "free" than "slave." When they could do so, they escaped and became "free" in fact, if not in law. Those who were legally free so often confronted the bitter truth that their "freedom" left them unable to find gainful employment, or a decent home in which to raise their families, or anything approaching equal treatment in the eyes of the law. "Freedom" without the chance to enjoy the fundamental rights of citizenship was not slavery, but it was not full freedom.

To be free and black was to be "in between" in many ways. In some instances it meant being of mixed race, but light skin was no hallmark of free status. The intermingling of peoples of African, European, and Native American descent had happened from the time the first Europeans established permanent colonies in North America. Liberty and light skin did not go hand in hand, except in the case of individuals who were so close to being white that they slipped across the racial divide, becoming not only free but white. Compounding the issue of racial identification was the lack of agreement among whites about exactly what constituted "black" and "white." In some instances, having one black grandparent made an individual black, at least in the eyes of the law. In other instances, descent was traced back to one's great-grandparents. "Freedom," though, had nothing to do with ancestry, unless one could prove descent from a free woman. Law codes invariably decreed that children inherited the status of their mothers. Thus the offspring of a dark-skinned free woman were free, while those born of the union of a light-skinned slave and her white owner were slaves unless and until their father chose to liberate them. And the existence of light-skinned slaves meant that on occasion white people fell victim to slave catchers and ended up in bondage.

If to dwell "in between" was not about appearance and ancestry for most free people of color, what was it about? Simply put, it was about status. It was about how the majority population was willing to let them live. Whites routinely regulated what free black people could and could not do. Regulation took the form of laws and local ordinances. The lists of prohibitions grew longer over time and encompassed everything from voting to owning a dog or walking with a cane ("unless in case of bodily infirmity," as a South Carolina law stipulated) or smoking a cigar in public. "Free" persons might have to register and pay a special tax for the privilege of remaining in the community where they had been born. If they left, they could perhaps never return. These laws endured in the American South long after the Civil War had ended and long after "free people of color" had ceased to constitute a separate class in society. In many instances, these laws served as the basis of the Black Codes and the Jim Crow legislation that governed the lives of black people during Reconstruction and beyond. There was an obvious logic to this. Once slavery was dead, it seemed only right that the laws that had evolved over centuries of black-white interaction should apply to the entire black population now that all African Americans were free. Even more ominous was the specter of white violence, which sought to enforce "appropriate" behavior on the part of free blacks, and racial violence was as common an occurrence in the North and Midwest as it was in the South.

From early colonial days liberty for black people invariably meant something different—something less—than it did for white people. It was a halfway freedom, in that it was not slavery but it was not the freedom that white people thought appropriate for themselves. In that respect it illustrated fundamental contradictions in American life, and not only in those areas where slavery lasted longest as a labor system. Decades after slavery had ended in the New England states, for instance, white residents often delivered to black people salutary reminders that they should "know their place"—and that "place" was not one of equality with whites.

My goal in *Between Slavery and Freedom* is to probe the ill-defined space between black freedom and white freedom in America from the early colonial era to the Civil War. The location of the boundary markers differed quite dramatically according to time and place. We have to jettison the notion that to be free and black meant the same thing wherever and whenever one lived. We are exploring a dozen generations of black people as they confronted the complex challenges of living somewhere in between lifelong servitude and the kind of freedom that white Americans regarded as their birthright. Life in Virginia in that colony's early days was not the same for blacks—or for whites—as it was in Massachusetts in the midst of the Revolution or in California in the era of the Gold Rush. It was not the same in the French and Spanish and Dutch settlements in North America that would eventually become part of the United States. And yet, in each of those settings, and in many different ways, black people struggled to secure for themselves nothing less than the full measure of freedom that they considered their due. They could *exist* "in between" liberty and bondage, but they were determined to *live* in freedom.

The story of black freedom in America begins in the Spanish outposts in Florida and the American Southwest in the 1500s and runs through to the Civil War and beyond. The first chapter of *Between Slavery and Freedom*, "Property or Persons," covers a broad span of time—over two-and-a-half centuries—a wide swath of territory, and a complex mix of cultures as waves of Spanish colonizers, and then their French, Dutch, and English rivals, imported hundreds of thousands of Africans to labor for them in perpetuity, and as those Africans and their American-born descendants fought back to try to claim their freedom. For a brief time it seemed that the American Revolution might usher in liberty for all, regardless of race. Chapter 2, "In Liberty's Cause," looks at how and why some blacks won their freedom during and immediately after the Revolution, even as the promises of "life, liberty and the pursuit of happiness" remained unfulfilled for the majority of black people.

Chapter 3, "Race, Liberty, and Citizenship in the New Nation," centers on the growth of America's free black population between 1790 and 1820. Slavery died in some parts of the United States and gained a new lease on life in others, but nowhere did freedom result in equality for black Americans. They were determined to see that it did, though. Chapter 4, "We Will Have Our Rights," carries the narrative forward to the next generation, whose members came of age between 1820 and 1850. Individually and collectively, free men and women struggled to advance the antislavery cause, while maintaining their own freedom and insisting on their entitlement as Americans to share fully in all of the opportunities that the nation offered its white citizens. In the tension-filled decade after 1850, the focus of chapter 5, some free blacks questioned whether they even had a future in America, especially when the nation's highest court declared that they had "no rights which the white man is bound to respect." But if some chose exile, many more chose to stay, confident that the nation *would* finally embrace the principles of liberty and equality set forth in the Declaration of Independence. And if it took a war to achieve those lofty goals that was a war many of them were ready and willing to fight.

~

Timeline

1500s	Spanish establish settlements in North America and bring in many thousands of African slaves and a smaller number of free black people as soldiers, settlers, and craftsmen
1600s	French, Dutch, and British carve out colonies in North America and import enslaved Africans, some of whom eventually become free
1664	Britain takes over Dutch colony of New Netherlands, renames it New York, and ends Dutch practice of granting slaves "half-freedom"
1660s–	
1750s	Legal restrictions on free blacks in Britain's American colonies increase
1772	Verdict in *Somersett* case leads to false reports that Britain has outlawed slavery
1775	American Revolution begins. Virginia's royal governor offers freedom to slaves of rebel owners in return for military service Prince Hall and other free black men in Boston organize the first black Masonic Lodge
1777	Vermont becomes the first state to prohibit slavery
1780	Pennsylvania passes Gradual Abolition Act
1783	Ruling in *Quock Walker* case that slavery violates the Massachusetts constitution
1784	Connecticut and Rhode Island pass gradual abolition laws

1787	Formation of Free African Society in Philadelphia
1791	African-American mathematician Benjamin Banneker challenges Thomas Jefferson regarding his views on black freedom
1793	Passage of first federal fugitive slave law. Some free blacks seized as alleged runaways
1799	Free black men in Philadelphia petition Congress to outlaw kidnapping of free people and begin abolishing slavery nationwide
	Congress refuses to receive their petition
1804	New Jersey passes gradual abolition act
	Ohio's "Black Code" imposes harsh restrictions on free blacks
1806	Opening of Boston's African Meeting House
1807	United States outlaws the trans-Atlantic slave trade as of January 1, 1808
1808	Northern free blacks start observing January 1 in the hope that ending the slave trade means slavery itself will soon end
	Observances cease by 1830 as disillusionment sets in
1814	Free men of color in New Orleans join Andrew Jackson in fighting off the British Army
1816	American Colonization Society (ACS) founded to encourage free people to leave America for Africa
1817	Free blacks in the North and Upper South begin protesting against the ACS
1818	Illinois outlaws slavery, but (1819) limits rights of free blacks
1821	New York restricts black voting rights
	ACS founds the colony of Liberia in West Africa and begins recruiting settlers
1822	Free black craftsman Denmark Vesey heads a conspiracy in Charleston, South Carolina, to destroy slavery. South Carolina enacts a series of repressive laws
1824	Anti-black violence in Providence, Rhode Island
Mid-1820s	Thousands of free blacks leave for Haiti. Most eventually return to the United States
1826	Race riot in Boston
1827	First black-owned newspaper, *Freedom's Journal*, published in New York City
	Emancipation of all remaining slaves in New York
1829	In Boston David Walker publishes his *Appeal to the Coloured Citizens of the World*

	Race riot in Cincinnati, Ohio. Many black residents leave for Canada
1830	In Philadelphia, Bishop Richard Allen chairs the first black national convention
1832	Boston's Maria W. Stewart becomes the first African-American woman to lecture in public to both men and women. She speaks on black rights and women's rights
1834	Racial unrest in New York City and Philadelphia In Canterbury, Connecticut, harassment from local whites forces Prudence Crandall to close her school for "young ladies and little misses of color"
1835	African-American men lose voting rights in North Carolina
1837	*Colored American* newspaper begins publication in New York City
1838	Pennsylvania disfranchises African Americans
1840s	Southerners protest when several Northern states pass "personal liberty laws" giving black people arrested as fugitives more opportunities to prove that they are in fact free
1841	Black men in Rhode Island regain voting rights lost in 1822
1842	Three-day race riot in Philadelphia
1845	Texas enters the Union as a slave state and passes laws to control free black people
1850	Passage of a harsher federal fugitive slave law sparks fears that free black people will be kidnapped and enslaved
1852	Black writer Martin R. Delany urges free people to rethink their opposition to emigration
1855	Massachusetts enacts a school integration law
1857	U.S. Supreme Court declares in the *Dred Scott* case that black people have no rights that whites are "bound to respect"
1859	Arkansas expels its entire free black population
1860	Restrictions on free black people increase in Southern states
1861	Civil War begins. Free black men volunteer for military service throughout the North and West but the U.S. government refuses to let them enlist

CHAPTER ONE

~

Property or Persons

Black Freedom in Colonial America, 1513–1770

Over the two-and-a-half centuries from the founding of the first permanent European colony in North America to the beginning of the American Revolution, hundreds of thousands of black people arrived on this continent. Many Europeans set sail for America in the colonial era to escape abject poverty, religious or ethnic persecution, or the prospect of the gallows. Even the least free—indentured servants who had agreed to work for a period of time in return for passage to America, or criminals who had traded death sentences for transportation to the colonies—could anticipate that one day they would be at liberty to make a new start on a new continent. Not so black women and men. While some came voluntarily and seized the opportunities the New World offered, most crossed the Atlantic as slaves, with no prospect of freedom, and none for their American-born descendants. Bondage in perpetuity was to be *their* reality in America, unless they could find a way to "remake" themselves as free people. The nature of black freedom and the routes to that freedom varied greatly over time and space in colonial America. Blacks searched constantly for the weak places in the slave systems the different European and colonial governments had devised, determined to transform themselves from "property" to "people."

The Spanish made their first foray to the mainland of North America in 1513. Within a couple of decades they were carving out settlements and bringing in both black and white people to make them profitable and productive. The different sets of circumstances under which black people came to North America in the service of the Spanish determined how they

1

fared. Free black men, who already spoke Spanish and had lived for years in Spain itself or on the Spanish Caribbean islands of Hispaniola or Cuba, came as soldiers, artisans, and interpreters. With the white conquistadors they trekked across the American Southeast and Southwest in search of the fabled Fountain of Youth and the Seven Cities of Gold. Like some of the white men they served with, an unknown number eventually settled as free farmers on the fringes of the vast Spanish Empire, intermarrying with Native American or black women.

These men and their families were the fortunate ones. Most black people in Spain's American dominions were slaves. The Spanish made extensive use of slave labor in the Caribbean and South and Central America, and they soon introduced the system to North America. They were as brutal in their exploitation of Africans and their descendants as any of their colonial rivals. Spanish law did, however, confer upon the enslaved some rights. The medieval Spanish code known as the *Siete Partidas* (Seven-Part Law) required masters to pay attention to their slaves' physical and spiritual welfare. More importantly, it offered slaves a path to freedom.

Under the principle of *coartación*, a slave could ask the authorities to name a price for his liberty, and his owner had to agree to it. Once a slave had scraped together part of his purchase price, he could hire himself out a few hours each week and earn more money. A larger payment gained the slave the right to move away from his owner's home. More freedoms came with more money, until the day when the slave paid the price in full and became a free person.

Throughout Spanish North America, in Texas and California, and most especially in Florida, slaves achieved their freedom in other ways as well. Relatively few white women came to the Spanish colonies, so white men routinely cohabited with enslaved women. The law forbade it, and so did the Catholic Church, but slaveholding merchants and planters ignored the secular and religious authorities when it came to their private lives. In some instances, they freed their concubines and their children and provided for them financially. Other slaves got their liberty because of their skills as craftsmen. Slave artisans were much more likely than field hands to be able to earn enough money to start the process of *coartación*. They might in time be able to buy not only themselves but their wives and children.

Other black men in Spanish territory fought their way to freedom. In 1565, Spain established the settlement of St. Augustine in Florida. The authorities quickly realized that to protect their beleaguered outpost from Native attacks, they had to call upon every able-bodied man, regardless of race. Thus they turned to their slaves, promising them freedom in return for military service. What began as a short-term survival tactic resulted in the creation of a sizable free black and *pardo* (mixed-race) fighting force. Wherever the Spanish founded settlements, sooner or later they recruited their slaves to help defend those settlements, and they accepted the reality that no man would risk his life if he knew he had to remain a slave. Military service led to freedom. Eventually the authorities in Florida organized their free black and *pardo* soldiers into formal military companies. Although the Spanish tried to keep these forces under white control, they could not do so. Black and mixed-race men rose through the ranks to become officers, and they led the men under their command into battle with the enemies of Spain. In the process, they claimed many of the same rights that other Spanish subjects enjoyed, insisting that their courage and loyalty entitled them to nothing less.

By the middle of the eighteenth century the black and *pardo* population of Spanish North America was a complex one. While Spain's slave system was undeniably brutal, it was loose enough to allow some people to gain their freedom. Throughout Spanish territory African and African-American men and women maneuvered, negotiated, and fought their way out of slavery. Those who became free began seeking ways to prosper as landowners, as business owners, and in some instances as slave owners.

While the Spanish were asserting their rights to all of North America, other Europeans were making *their* presence felt on the continent. Their settlements also relied, to varying degree, on the labor of enslaved black people. In the late seventeenth and early eighteenth centuries the French spread steadily north from the Gulf of Mexico and south from Canada down the Mississippi. In the vast Louisiana Territory, French colonists engaged in raising sugar cane in the swampy, humid lands around the Mississippi Delta, cultivating grain in the Midwest (the so-called "Illinois Country"), and trading furs for European manufactured goods with Native peoples. With a constant need for workers, settlers enslaved Indians. They also brought in black slaves from Africa and the West Indies. Regardless of the race of their slaves, French settlers treated them with appalling cruelty. They met every act of rebellion or defiance, real or imagined, with savage reprisals.

Securing one's freedom in French territories proved more difficult than in Spanish territories, in part because there was no French equivalent of *coartación*. A slave could attempt to bargain for his or her freedom, but a master or mistress had no obligation to agree to any kind of arrangement. Theoretically, the French slave system did not allow slaves to own property or earn money, hence depriving them of the means to purchase their liberty. In practice, though, some slaves *were* able to buy themselves. The port of

New Orleans, for instance, could never attract enough skilled white artisans. That spelled opportunity for slaves whose masters arranged for them to be trained in a specific trade and then permitted them to hire their time. Cohabitation was also as common in French settlements as it was in Spanish ones. Some Frenchmen took Native American "wives." Others took enslaved women as their "housekeepers," and in some instances they freed them. And, like the Spanish, the French recognized the wisdom of employing black men as soldiers, and granting them freedom for their service.

In 1729, the French in and around New Orleans began freeing some of their slaves and arming them to help repel attacks by the Natchez Indians. The black soldiers met a vital need and fought well. Yet the French were no more committed to freedom than the Spanish, but did what they had to for their own security. As the influence of the black troops increased with every challenge to French power in the region, the authorities found they could not do without them. Eventually French colonial administrators followed the lead of the Spanish and organized the soldiers into military companies commanded by their own officer corps. The soldiers, and especially their officers, became not only free but in some instances wealthy.

Once France began acquiring colonies and importing black people to labor in them, the French king and his ministers crafted a series of laws that set down the rights and obligations of masters and slaves. The so-called *Code Noir* (Black Code) concentrated power in the hands of white slave-holders and made slaves subservient in basically every aspect of their lives. Theoretically, there were two classes in the colonies, white slave owners and black slaves, but the *Code Noir* did not entirely ignore the presence of a third class, the *gens de couleur libres*, or free people of color.

Although the *Code Noir* forbade interracial cohabitation and marriage, the authorities in France tacitly admitted that white men were living with black and mixed-race women and that those relationships were producing children whom their fathers might, if they were so inclined, set free. They also acknowledged that slaves were finding other ways to get their freedom. A free population existed and they needed to determine the status of that population.

Not surprisingly, the *Code Noir* tried to prevent free blacks from aiding and abetting slaves in rebelling or escaping. *Gens de couleur* who sheltered runaway slaves risked heavy fines, and if they could not pay them they could lose their own freedom. The *Code Noir* instructed former slaves always to show great respect to the white family that had been kind and generous enough to free them and warned them that any sign of disrespect would result in harsh punishment. However—and this was a provision unlike that in any of the other European colonies in North America—the *Code Noir* also declared that the King of France granted "to manumitted slaves the same rights, privileges and immunities . . . enjoyed by free-born persons . . . not only with regard to their persons, but also to their property."[1] The *Code Noir* at least implied that ex-slaves would enjoy a certain measure of equality with whites once they ceased to be slaves.

It was one thing for the king across the ocean to declare what should and should not happen in his distant colonies. It was quite another to put those declarations into practice. Despite what the *Code Noir* said, one's "rights, privileges and immunities" often depended on the color of one's skin. Full equality did not prevail throughout the Louisiana Territory, although it is fair to say that in some of the French settlements free people of African ancestry did enjoy a higher status than their brothers and sisters in the British colonies. However, it would be incorrect to claim that the situation of free people of color in French North America was better than it was anywhere else or that white racial attitudes were any more benign.

In the colonial era time and place determined just what free black people could do and indeed what opportunities they had to become free. That was not only the case in French and Spanish territories, but in all of the thirteen British colonies. The slaves would have to rely on luck, determination, and courage to gain their liberty, and free blacks would have to be equally resourceful to hold on to it. Slavery took root more quickly in some of Britain's colonies than in others, but within a generation the institution existed in all of them, along with a patchwork of laws and practices that kept most black people from achieving freedom.

The white planters who converged on the wharf of Jamestown, Virginia in the summer of 1619 to inspect an enterprising Dutch captain's human cargo were not personally familiar with slavery. They knew, though, that the Spanish practiced it, and that the Dutch and the Portuguese were competing with one another to keep Spain's colonies throughout the Americas fully stocked with slaves. They also knew that for decades some of their countrymen had been trying to muscle their way into the African trade. A few of the Virginia planters had seen black people because some aristocratic households in England had acquired them as dependents or servants. What exactly those early white Virginians thought about darker-skinned people is a subject that has intrigued historians for decades. Certainly the thought uppermost in the minds of the planters that day in 1619 was that here was an excellent opportunity to solve their most pressing problem, namely the labor shortage. They could never get enough white indentured servants from Britain, or hold on to those they got for long enough to make a profit, and they were uneasy about the idea of coercing Native Americans into working for them. It was impractical and it was dangerous in a region where Indians vastly outnumbered whites. The Dutch captain offered them a "parcel" of Africans they could purchase and send into the fields to cultivate the tobacco on which the colony's prosperity depended.

Given the economic and social patterns that had developed in Virginia by the mid-eighteenth century, it is tempting to assume that the English planters bought all of the Africans on that unidentified Dutch ship as slaves, that they kept them in lifelong bondage, that they continued buying African slaves as more ships arrived in their ports, and that slavery emerged as a fully developed labor system almost immediately. That is a highly inaccurate picture, though, and represents the dangers of judging one era by the customs and practices of another. The Virginia that George Washington and Thomas Jefferson knew in the 1750s and 1760s was not the Virginia that the planters of the 1620s and 1630s knew or that the colony's earliest black settlers knew.

Laboring long hours without pay was certainly something those first black immigrants to Virginia experienced, but it was not what every one of them endured for the rest of their days. African Anthony Johnson, for instance, arrived on another Dutch ship one year after that first cargo of slaves struggled ashore in Jamestown. He gained his freedom—how we do not know—acquired land, and married a free black woman. Anthony and Mary Johnson raised their children in freedom and purchased black slaves as well as the services of white indentured workers. The Johnsons were not alone. Up and down Virginia's Eastern Shore there were several dozen free black farmers in that first generation or two of settlement who were free because they had bought their way out of bondage, usually by raising their own crops of tobacco on their masters' land and using that tobacco as currency in what was essentially a barter economy.

Those early free African people and their American-born children interacted on many levels with English settlers. They traded with them, fought with them, slept with them, and labored alongside them. However, at least some of the influential white men in the colony were uneasy about their presence. These black people were free, but somehow their blackness made them *different*. The law codes Virginia's House of Burgesses drew up in the 1660s spelled that out, declaring that free black people "ought not in all respects . . . [to] be admitted to a full fruition of the exemptions and impunities of the English."[2] This was very different indeed from the statement in the *Code Noir* about the "privileges and immunities" that all free people were entitled to, regardless of race.

The sons and grandsons of the planters who had come down to the James River in 1619 to inspect the Dutch captain's cargo were hungry for more land and more labor to stay competitive, and they demanded cheap labor from workers they could treat as brutally as they chose. They were far less reluctant than their fathers and grandfathers had been to enslave Native Americans. Increasingly, though, they turned to black slaves, importing thousands each year from Africa and the Caribbean. White Virginians' insatiable appetite for slaves undermined the status of the free black community. New, more restrictive ordinances made it much more difficult for black people to bargain with their masters for their freedom, while the descendants of the Johnsons and other black people in the "founding" generation who were already free found their route to modest prosperity blocked at every turn.

The labor situation in the neighboring colony of Maryland was very similar to that in Virginia. Maryland's tobacco planters moved quickly from using white indentured servants, who were always in short supply, to buying slaves. They could not afford to buy many in the early days of settlement, and they often worked their farms with a mix of white bound servants and black and Native American slaves. As they grew wealthier, though, they opted for slaves, and increasingly they chose black slaves over captive Indians.

Gaining one's freedom in Maryland and Virginia was never easy, but it became much more difficult as time wore on. Nothing obliged an owner to free a slave, not conversion to Christianity, mastery of the English language, or even ties of kinship. In both colonies a child followed the condition of his or her mother. If a white man fathered children with a slave, those children became slaves. It was a different story when a child was born to a white woman and an enslaved black man. Although both colonies passed laws to try to prevent such relationships, they did occur. Initially Maryland's lawmakers took a tougher stance than their counter-parts in Virginia, decreeing in 1664 that if any "free borne woman shall inter marry with any slave . . . [she] shall Serve the master of such slave dureing [sic] the life of her husband."[3] That is what happened to at least one white woman, Eleanor Butler. When "Irish Nell" wed a slave, Charles, she joined him in servitude. Their children were slaves from birth. Then Maryland changed the law and made the status of the mother the status of her child. Ultimately, Eleanor and Charles's descendants sued for their freedom and won. Not only in Maryland and Virginia but throughout British North America descent from a white woman generally resulted in freedom, although proving one's ancestry to the satisfaction of the courts presented enormous difficulties. And freedom came with a hefty price. The courts might declare that a child was free, but then order that child bound out to service for many years and the mother whipped or fined for, in the words of a Virginia law, engaging in "abominable" behavior that resulted in the creation of a "spurious issue."[4]

Several factors determined the situation of people of African descent in the region to the south of Maryland and Virginia. What are today North and South Carolina were originally two halves of one huge colony that King Charles II granted to a powerful group of Englishmen in 1663. They named it Carolina, *Carolus* being the Latin for Charles, in his honor. From the beginning, the Proprietors of Carolina were committed to African slavery. Several invested heavily in Britain's Royal African Company and engaged in battling the Dutch and the French for control of the major West African slaving ports. At least a couple had financial interests in the emerging plantation systems in Britain's West Indian colonies.

The English who settled in what became North Carolina were happy to purchase black people as slaves. But because the economy took time to flourish, they simply lacked the means to acquire as many as they would have liked. Eventually, the settlers grew wealthy from growing tobacco, raising cattle, and supplying the Royal Navy and private shipyards with hemp, pitch, turpentine, and timber. Before long, the wealthier settlers were expanding the size of their workforce by buying additional slaves, generally from planters and traders in Virginia. The enslaved used every strategy they could to gain their freedom. They fled to the Indian tribes of the region, or took refuge with poor backcountry farmers who, so they hoped, might shelter anyone willing to work for little more than their keep. Others cultivated small patches of land and sold the produce or worked at a skilled trade, while bargaining with their owners to purchase themselves. Every strategy had its perils. An owner might cheat a slave out of his money and refuse to free him. A backcountry farmer might exploit and enslave a desperate runaway. Even adoption into an Indian tribe might not lead to lifelong freedom. When tribes made treaties with the British they often had to agree to hand back fugitive slaves. Whatever the risks, though, the enslaved were willing to take them. Some did succeed in gaining their liberty, and although it came with restrictions, it was vastly preferable to lifelong enslavement.

Many of the earliest white immigrants to South Carolina came not directly from Britain but from Britain's Caribbean colonies, principally Barbados. The Proprietors lured them with offers of free land, and they came in considerable numbers, bringing with them the black slaves they already owned. They were eager to get more slaves, and when the chance arose, they bought Indians. In South Carolina, at least until the early 1700s, enslaved Africans and Indians toiled on the same plantations. Within a generation, racial lines became blurred as Englishmen fathered children with their African- and Native-American slaves, and the enslaved themselves formed unions that produced offspring who shared the heritage of both parents.

White South Carolinians put their slaves to all kinds of work, from felling trees to raising cattle and cultivating sugar cane. Some planters did well, but timber, sugar, and livestock did not earn enough to make the colony as a whole economically successful. They turned to rice and indigo, staple crops that provided profits to buy more African slaves, whom they considered best suited to the backbreaking labor these crops required. The port of Charleston became a major hub of the Atlantic slave trade. By 1710, black people, the overwhelming majority of them enslaved, far outnumbered whites in South Carolina.

Despite the pervasiveness of slavery, through the first century of South Carolina's existence some Africans and African Americans gained their freedom. Hundreds escaped, either alone or in small groups. A prime destination was Florida, where the Spanish welcomed them and let them settle in freedom, not because Spanish officials opposed slavery but because they saw this as a tactic to weaken their British enemies. They even encouraged the men to become soldiers, knowing they would fight courageously in the event of an English attack because their own liberty and that of their families was at stake.

While some slaves fled to Spanish territory to gain their freedom, others created independent "maroon" communities in parts of the colony they hoped were too remote for whites to find. Still others opted not for flight but for negotiation, seeing what an owner might accept in return for their liberty. Generally, though, the people who gained their liberty in South Carolina did so because of their close personal ties to whites. Many white men kept slave concubines, and while the law gave female slaves no rights, some masters did free their sexual partners and the children the women bore them. Occasionally they gave their "housekeepers" and their biracial progeny money, land, and even slaves. By the early 1700s, in and around Charleston, and less frequently on the plantations, a small class of mixed-race free people began to emerge.

Apart from those who were legally free, hundreds of other black people existed in the "shadowland" between lifelong servitude and freedom in South Carolina. Slaves whom their owners trusted to take goods to market and return with the proceeds had a remarkable degree of liberty. Enslaved craftsmen sometimes received permission to hire themselves out by the day, the week, or the month, although they had to hand over to their masters most of what they earned. While local laws and ordinances said one thing about slave mobility, in practice individual slave owners ignored the regulations if it was to their own advantage to do so.

By the 1750s and 1760s there were tens of thousands of black and mixed race people in South Carolina. A very small number had their legal freedom, and some even enjoyed a modest degree of wealth. However, the majority of South Carolinians of African ancestry were condemned to unrelenting toil. Their only hope lay in rebellion or flight.

Unlike South Carolina, Georgia, established in 1732, initially outlawed slavery. The founders hoped to make the colony a place where some of the less fortunate members of English society could start over. The Trustees proposed to ship them and their families to Georgia, give them land so that they could become economically self-sufficient, and rely on them to keep the Spanish in Florida at bay. However, white settlers soon learned what the Trustees did not tell them: working the land in a hot, steamy, disease-inducing climate was far from easy. Before long, Georgians were insisting on having slaves and pressuring the Trustees to lift the ban on slave ownership. It took almost two decades, but eventually the settlers prevailed. By the time of the Revolution Georgia was a slightly poorer and less well-developed replica of South Carolina, with gangs of slaves living short, wretched lives in the swampy lowlands to produce rice, the "white gold" that put the youngest of Britain's North American colonies on the path to becoming one of its richest.

A few of Georgia's slaves succeeded in becoming free. Some did so by fleeing to Florida, just as the Trustees had warned they would. Others took refuge with Native peoples, intermarried with them, and in a few short years transformed themselves culturally and linguistically into Cherokees and Choctaws, Creeks and Seminoles. Those who actually remained in the colony and secured their liberty generally did so, as did their counterparts in South Carolina, through ties of affection or blood to white owners. In both colonies, maintaining one's freedom required constant vigilance. Whites assumed that every black man or woman was a slave unless he or she could present overwhelming proof to the contrary.

Slavery was not confined to the South in the colonial period or to those areas where white settlers needed workers to grow staples like tobacco, rice, and indigo. The three Mid-Atlantic colonies of Pennsylvania, New Jersey, and New York were different in many respects from the colonies of the South, and those differences fundamentally shaped the lives and the expectations of the region's black residents. Not only was the labor they performed different, but so were the chances they had to extricate themselves from bondage. What was not different, though, was that slavery was a fact of life. Most whites accepted it, and did not have much use for free black people, whom they generally considered troublesome and lazy. Any suggestion that freedom should confer on black people the same fundamental rights that whites enjoyed provoked anger, derisive laughter, or simply disbelief.

In 1664, when the British took over the colony of New Netherland from the Dutch and renamed it New York, they found themselves coping with black people who were neither enslaved nor free. This part of the Dutch legacy was something with which the British were decidedly uncomfortable. The Dutch had been as ready as any of the other European colonizers to use slave labor when they came to North America in the early 1600s. In the first generation of settlement they had shipped thousands of slaves from Africa and the Caribbean to New Netherland. Some they had employed in their households and on their farms, others they had sent to labor on the wharves in the port of New Amsterdam (today's New York City) loading and unloading their trading vessels. By the 1640s, though, they had another use for at least some of their slaves. Violence between the colonists and the Native peoples of the Manhattan area was escalating, which led the Dutch to extend "half-freedom" to some enslaved men. Purely from motives of self-interest they settled those men on land between the white settlement of Manhattan and the Indian lands and modified the conditions of their servitude to give them an incentive to fight the Indians, rather than unite with them. The half-free lived and farmed independently and had the right to keep any money they earned. In return for their privileged position they had to make an annual payment to the ruling Dutch West India Company. These half-free men struggled to secure the freedom of their wives and, despite what the Company said about half-freedom not being hereditary, they explored every avenue to make sure their children were free.

After New Netherland changed hands, the British not only renamed the colony but dispensed with the institution of half-freedom. They instinctively distrusted black people who occupied a position in between slavery and full freedom. They worried about the numbers claiming half-free status. The half-free were much too independent-minded and the authorities suspected that they were sheltering runaway slaves on their small farms. Step by step, the new British regime undermined the position of the half-free, especially their ownership of land. They drew lines of demarcation between themselves and both free and enslaved blacks. For example, after 1697 no person of African descent, regardless of status, could be buried in the same graveyard as whites, hence the origin of New York's long-lost and recently rediscovered African Burial Ground. Whites did not want black people too close to them, even in death, and they certainly did not want black mourners traipsing across *their* final resting places.

Following the brutal suppression of a slave uprising in New York City in 1712, piecemeal legislation gave way to the wholesale reworking of the laws relating to black people. The new code applied to the free, the half-free, and the enslaved. It had not escaped the notice of the authorities that at least one of those accused of instigating the uprising, "Peter the Doctor," was a free man. Under the new law, free people could not own any real estate. It also became difficult and expensive for owners to free their slaves because they now had to pay a heavy financial penalty for the privilege of doing so. Blacks in bondage had a place in the grand scheme of things, but those who were free most definitely did not.

The situation was much the same in New Jersey. Slaves were present in appreciable numbers, especially in the eastern part of the colony, by the last decades of the seventeenth century. The growth of New York City resulted in a constant demand for food. East Jersey's farmers made good money keeping the expanding metropolis fed, and they used some of that money to buy slaves. West Jersey had fewer slaves because its farms were smaller and more isolated and the need for labor was less pressing. Generally, though, whites in both sections of New Jersey displayed little reluctance to acquire slaves when they had the means to do so. They did not welcome the creation of a significant free black population. In their minds, freedmen and women posed a continual threat to white authority. New Jersey lawmakers responded to that unease created by the presence of free blacks by placing restrictions on the securing of freedom very similar to those in force in New York.

Those blacks in New Jersey who succeeded in extricating themselves from slavery faced a daily battle simply to survive. By law, they could not own land. It was impossible, though, to prevent them from trying to find some small patch on which they could plant crops and raise livestock, even if they had to resort to squatting on land that no one else seemed to want. In coastal areas and along the rivers they fished. Away from the water they hunted small game. Those who had trades tried to practice them. Generally, however, they were condemned to poverty, and they confronted the unpalatable truth that whites assumed they were slaves unless they could prove otherwise. New Jersey had one of the harshest slave codes of any of the northern colonies for the simple reason that it had so many slaves—almost 12 percent of its overall population by the 1770s. Free people lived on the margins in colonial New Jersey, literally and figuratively. One false step and they could find themselves back in bondage.

To the south of New Jersey, most of Pennsylvania's Quaker colonists had no misgivings whatsoever about importing Africans and profiting from their unpaid labor. The colony's founder, William Penn, was at first perturbed about the morality of slave ownership. However, he soon gave way, and even acquired several slaves himself. In 1684, just three years after Pennsylvania received its royal charter, the slaver *Isabella* docked in the Delaware River with 150 Africans on board, and white settlers vied with one another to buy them. Further shipments soon followed. Within a generation, black slaves were a common sight on the streets of Philadelphia. Although a few whites condemned human bondage as a sin, most were happy to purchase a slave or two. Slaves did almost every conceivable type of labor. In the country-side they worked on farms, in homes, and in all kinds of rural industries, most notably the iron foundries that sprang up to exploit Pennsylvania's mineral wealth. Slaves moved back and forth between the countryside and the city. Philadelphia newspapers often carried advertisements describing a particular woman or man as "fit for all manner of Town or Country Work."[5] Pennsylvania's slaves were expected to be versatile, and many of them were.

Pennsylvania did not lag far behind her sister colonies when it came to regulating the status of free blacks—and over the years some slaves did succeed in becoming free, most through self-purchase. The colony's "black codes" told those people with whom they could trade and whom they could welcome into their homes. Aiding a suspected runaway, buying goods from a slave (which he or she was presumed to have stolen), or selling alcohol to a slave could put a free person's own liberty in jeopardy. Most white Pennsylvanians wished the colony did not have a single free black inhabitant. They believed they were, in the words of the preamble to a 1751 law, an "idle and slothful people." There were too many of them, and they had a worrisome tendency to congregate in Philadelphia, where (so lawmakers alleged) they rented small hovels and shacks and generally annoyed white people by their presence.[6] Whatever whites thought and feared, though, there were only about fifty free black families in Philadelphia by the 1770s, and perhaps the same number scattered throughout the counties adjoining the city—some 500–600 individuals in all. They took whatever employment they could, struggled to keep their heads above water financially, and tried not to fall foul of the law. It was a tough existence, made tougher by the knowledge that they and their children could be bound out to labor if the authorities judged them to be vagrants or paupers.

Just as slavery flourished in the Mid-Atlantic colonies, so it took root in New England. The tendency of masters throughout the region to refer to both hired hands and slaves as "servants" makes it difficult to determine precisely how many slaves there were in any neighborhood at any point in time. It also hides the presence of black people who were free, who earned wages, and were indeed "servants."

The Puritans of Massachusetts gave legal sanction to slavery early in the colony's history. The 1641 Body of Liberties ruled that it was lawful to hold as property "Captives taken in just warres," those who voluntarily sold themselves into bondage, and those who were sold into slavery by others.[7] Obviously that covered every category of individuals the Puritans might lay claim to. Within fifty years black slaves were "fixtures" not only in port towns like Boston but in rural areas. Some came directly from West Africa and others from the British colonies in the West Indies. Massachusetts never had the large gangs of slaves one would see in the South or even in the Mid-Atlantic colonies, and there were plenty of white householders who could simply not justify the purchase of a single slave. Nevertheless, black slavery emerged as part of the fabric of social and economic life in colonial Massachusetts. Black freedom, however, did not.

Rhode Islanders were even more eager than their Massachusetts neighbors to acquire slaves. There was a fleeting attempt in the 1650s to limit the period of servitude to ten years, but it went nowhere. The pressure for cheap labor on farms, in private homes, and in the bustling town of Newport was simply too great, and the town's merchants soon enmeshed themselves in the trans-Atlantic slave trade. By 1770, Rhode Island, the smallest of the New England colonies, had the highest percentage of slaves. Its free black population, by contrast, numbered just a few hundred individuals, and the colony's laws, combined with prevailing white assumptions about people of color, left them struggling to maintain their freedom.

Slavery also flourished in Connecticut. Thriving coastal communities were hungry for labor, and slaves supplied it. Slaves accounted for a significant percentage of farmhands, especially in the eastern part of the colony. They did other kinds of work as well. Depending on age and gender, they were blacksmiths and wheelwrights, dairymaids and household drudges. They planted and wormed tobacco, and enslaved black men built, maintained, loaded and helped crew every kind of vessel that sailed out of Connecticut's ports, from small coasting skiffs, to brigs and schooners in the West Indian trade, and much larger square-riggers plying the trans-Atlantic routes. Although by the end of the colonial period Rhode Island had the highest ratio of slaves to whites, Connecticut had the largest number slaves in New England—nearly 6,500. Its free black population was very small in comparison to the number of enslaved blacks—perhaps 300 people in all.

Further north, New Hampshire law recognized and protected slavery. Once Portsmouth began to grow as a port, merchants shipped in slaves. Black men provided much-needed labor, skilled and semi-skilled, while the white families that prospered through trade bought black women as household "help." Other coastal communities sprang up, and the more affluent whites in those communities purchased slaves. And even though they were a rarity in the area that would eventually become Vermont, several hundred enslaved black people were there by the beginning of the eighteenth century, struggling to survive, and pushing at the boundaries between slavery and freedom.

Although the majority of black New Englanders were slaves for life, a small minority gained their freedom. In some instances they became free against their will. Connecticut, Massachusetts, and Rhode Island all passed restrictions on which slaves an owner could emancipate and how much that owner had to pay for the privilege of doing so. Lawmakers worried less about the inhumanity of a slaveholder abandoning people who were too old or too infirm to support themselves and more about how much the maintenance of such helpless ex-slaves would cost their locality. Those same concerns occupied the minds of the enslaved, some of whom rejected outright the offer of emancipation. Freedom when it came in one's old age could prove a curse rather than a blessing if it meant being turned loose to starve or die of exposure in the harsh New England winter.

All of the New England colonies found ways to discourage free black people, young or old, from settling within their borders. In 1717, for instance, Connecticut passed a law forbidding freedmen and women from remaining in any town where whites objected to their presence. They were also prohibited from buying land or opening a business. Some individuals managed to ingratiate themselves sufficiently to get grudging permission to stay in a particular community, but the laws remained on the books, a constant reminder that free black people did not have the same rights as their white neighbors. If they did get the consent to settle down, it would not be as free and independent people. With few chances to become self-supporting, they would have to work as farmhands or live-in servants for whites in a status of dependency that left them little better off than when they had been slaves. They could not get ahead financially because of the hostile laws, and then they had to endure criticism for not making better use of their liberty.

Communities in Massachusetts and Rhode Island routinely "warned out" or expelled anyone who was indigent or seemed likely to become a public charge. Town officials forced them over the boundary into the next town, which then hastily moved them on into a neighboring town until they had nowhere left to go. Admittedly white people as well as people of color felt the weight of these exclusionary practices, but free blacks did so with much greater frequency, and local officials less often gave them the benefit of the doubt when they insisted that they were doing the best they could under difficult circumstances. Free blacks were also much more likely to end up in the region's jails and poorhouses.

Black New Englanders struggled to make their way in the world. A few managed to buy or rent land and become independent farmers. They generated a paper trail in the form of wills and deeds, and their names also appeared on the tax rolls, often with the notation that they were black. In port towns like Boston and Newport, free people who had access to capital set themselves up as small-scale traders. Those who had mastered a skill as slaves tried to put that skill to use once they were free. Although some free craftsmen and women did prosper, many found it impossible to get customers once they were working for themselves and not for white masters. Generally, free people took work where they could find it. Black men went to sea as sailors, whalers, and fishermen. Black women labored as domestics, performing the same tasks that they had as slaves. Those free black men who married Native-American women, as some did, especially in southern New England, enmeshed themselves in complex kinship networks that brought them not only companionship but economic opportunities as they traded, farmed, and hunted with their new extended families. However, lack of money or credit, discriminatory laws, and a white community that viewed them with suspicion and outright hostility conspired to relegate most free black people to the margins of New England society.

When it came to formal education, few black people in any of the colonies made the transition from bondage to freedom with the ability to read and write. There were exceptions. Occasionally an owner saw it as a religious duty to ensure that his or her slaves could read the Scriptures. Most, though, believed that an educated slave was a dangerous slave. Admittedly there were regional variations. Where white literacy was higher, for instance in urban areas in New England, more black people were likely to be literate. In the countryside, especially the further south one went, there were plenty of white people who lived their whole lives without being able to sign their names, so understandably their slaves had no better access to literacy than they did. As soon as they were free and had the opportunity to do so, free people seized the chance to educate themselves and their children. To be able to sign one's name with something more than an X was for many a hallmark of freedom. Those who could read and write often taught their friends and family members. Sympathetic white ministers and priests sometimes organized classes and so did dedicated laypeople, like Philadelphia's Anthony Benezet.

Nowhere in any of the colonies, Spanish or French, Dutch or British, did a slave's conversion to Christianity entitle him or her to freedom. Some owners queried whether they would have to free any of their slaves who became Christians, and everywhere the churches, Protestant and Catholic, gave the same comforting answer. It was good to communicate one's Christian faith to one's slaves. In the case of Catholic owners, the Church urged them to let their slaves receive the sacraments. A Christian slave was still a slave, though. Some masters and mistresses did feel compelled to share their religious values with their slaves, and some slaves embraced one or other varieties of Christianity. However, having to occupy the separate "Negro pew" or "Negro gallery" in a church or meetinghouse and listen to tedious sermons that stressed obedience to one's earthly master did little to make a slave want to share in a faith that seemed anything but liberating.

The Great Awakening, a wave of religious fervor that swept the British colonies in the 1730s and 1740s, transformed some parts of the religious landscape and profoundly affected both the institution of slavery and black spiritual life. From their pulpits ministers urged the need for repentance and a "born again" experience. Itinerant preachers expanded upon that message and proclaimed that true believers had a divine obligation to bring into the Christian fold every member of their household, regardless of race or condition. Some slave owners listened. New religious groups appeared on the scene. Baptists and Methodists embraced, sometimes literally, their black brothers and sisters, while individual ministers and white laypeople made efforts to evangelize the black community. Of the older denominations, only the Society of Friends (Quakers) rejected slavery outright. A few Quakers had been preaching for years that slavery violated God's law. Most Friends ignored them, but a series of crises among Quakers in the 1750s led to a period of deep introspection and ultimately to a decision that one could not be both a Quaker and a slaveholder. Friends liberated their slaves and some actually compensated them for their years of unpaid toil. It was an important victory. It did not mean, however, that slavery was dead even in Pennsylvania, the heartland of Quakerism, nor did it necessarily imply a commitment to racial equality.

As the colonial era drew to a close, there were some glimmers of hope for some enslaved blacks that they might be able to make their way to freedom and for those who were already free that the future might be brighter for them and their freeborn children. In 1754, war broke out between Britain and France. As they had done in earlier years, the French turned to their slaves to help fill the ranks of fighting men. Bondsmen gained their liberty through military service, and the free black soldiers serving in the existing military companies proved once more their importance as defenders of French colonial interests. While the English were far more reluctant than the French, the Spanish and the Dutch to use their slaves as soldiers, and certainly they never organized anything like the black and mixed-race militia companies that existed in Louisiana and Florida, as the French and Indian War dragged on, black men did serve. Recruiters anxious to fill their quotas turned a blind eye as black men, some free and others undoubtedly runaways, turned up to enlist.

The war ended in a stinging defeat for France, with far-reaching repercussions in the realm of international politics. In 1763, hard-pressed by the British, the French king traded the entire Louisiana Territory to Spain. For the first time, slaves in the Territory could take advantage of the Spanish institution of *coartación*. The number of self-purchased free people, especially in and around New Orleans, rose significantly. However, the overwhelming majority of Africans and African Americans in the Louisiana Territory and in Spain's older settlements in North America reaped no benefit from the change from French to Spanish rule. They remained enslaved, as did an unknown number of black people in another piece of the once-great French empire. Under the terms of the treaty that ended the French and Indian War the British took over the Illinois Country, the land east of the Mississippi. Home to French farmers and traders for several generations, the region had never had a large enslaved population because most of the whites who lived there were too poor to buy even one slave, but some had the means to do so. The forced handover to Britain did nothing to ease the plight of the slaves of the Illinois Country, and a steady influx of white settlers from the older British colonies resulted in an increase in the slave population, since some of those settlers brought their human "property" with them to perform the backbreaking labor of clearing the land and carving out farms.

In all of the colonies the enslaved did as they had always done. They fled in droves, exploiting everything they could use to their advantage—their ability to speak different languages, their job skills, their talent for talking their way out of trouble, their knowledge of the lay of the land, and their ties of kinship or friendship to other slaves, to free blacks, to various Native peoples, and occasionally to whites. How many passed successfully into the free community is unknown. Safety and security lay in avoiding detection. Others tried to negotiate their way to freedom, offering money or a promise of faithful service in return for one day being free. And in a few instances they turned to the courts to sue for their liberty.

The Massachusetts Body of Liberties had extended to slaves in that colony in 1641 a right slaves did not have anywhere else in British North America, namely the right to initiate a lawsuit. With the help of a few liberal-minded white lawyers, some Massachusetts slaves looked for legal loopholes in the terms of their enslavement—a freeborn mother, an abusive master, a promise of freedom uttered and not honored—and they sued. Sometimes plaintiffs won and some of those who emerged victorious even secured damages for unlawful imprisonment. A few owners panicked, wondering how long it might be before one of their slaves took them to court, and the number of private manumissions rose slightly, but slavery survived in Massachusetts, as it did elsewhere in the British colonies.

For a brief while, though, it seemed that slavery was about to die throughout the whole of the British Empire. The enslaved hoped that was the case and many slaveholders feared they were justified in that hope. In London in the autumn of 1771, a slave by the name of James Somersett fled from his master, Charles Stewart. Stewart pursued Somersett, recaptured him, and put him in jail to await transportation to the West Indies. Somersett got word of his plight to members of the small but influential antislavery movement in the city and the group took the matter to court. In 1772, Lord Chief Justice Mansfield ruled that Stewart did not have the right under English Common Law to detain James Somersett and remove him from the kingdom against his will, since slaves in England had access to the justice system. It was a landmark decision. Although Mansfield did not outlaw slavery and he carefully spelled out that his verdict applied only to slaves in England, most people who heard about the verdict ignored its subtleties. In England black people and their white friends contended that all the slaves in the kingdom—some 15,000 individuals—were now free. Across the Atlantic newspapers were full of reports of slaves stowing away on ships bound for England.

Freedom remained the elusive goal of hundreds of thousands of Africans and African Americans, not only in the British colonies but throughout North America. Some slaves were more free than others. With their owners' permission they went off to sea for months at a time. They hired themselves out. They had masters and mistresses who allowed them certain privileges and treated them better than others did. In some communities, the enslaved actually enjoyed a few days of respite and merrymaking each year—as long as their owners felt confident that they could reassert control once the brief "holiday" was over. The enslaved were under no illusions, though. Whatever fleeting freedom they experienced as slaves, they wanted the freedom that came with belonging to no one but themselves.

Those who ultimately did make the transition from "property" to "persons" all too often discovered that their hard-won freedom did not guarantee them anything approaching equality with whites. Whatever the laws of a particular colony said—and most of them were very restrictive when it came to what free black people could and could not do—the attitudes of the majority community were even more important. What whites in a particular neighborhood might tolerate in the case of a free black man or woman they trusted would result in harassment or open violence in the case of someone they disliked or distrusted. And distrust of free black people was pervasive in colonial America. Rumors abounded about their alleged contempt for authority. In Rhode Island they were allegedly enticing slaves to gamble and carouse. In South Carolina "a Gang of Banditti" composed of "Mulattoes, Mustees and Free Negroes" was stealing horses.[8] In Virginia free people were inducing slaves to raid their owners' homes and plantations. In Pennsylvania they were helping their enslaved friends escape. In Massachusetts they were congregating in the streets of Boston and other towns after dark. In New York they were doing all sorts of things that threatened peace and good order. The litany of complaints went on and on and the demands for harsh new laws grew louder and more urgent during the course of the eighteenth century as the numbers of free people grew. Free blacks responded by refusing to become the victims of white fear and prejudice. They pushed back against attempts to reclaim them as slaves, deny them the chance to make a living, and render their freedom something far less than white people were accustomed to. By the time of the Revolution, free blacks were a force, albeit a small force, to be reckoned with in the British colonies and beyond.

CHAPTER TWO

~

In Liberty's Cause

Black Freedom in Revolutionary America, 1770–1790

Black people fought for their freedom on many fronts in the era of independence. Most obviously and directly, they offered their aid on the battlefield and behind the lines to whoever would guarantee them their liberty. The tumultuous years leading up to the Revolution also witnessed an ideological battle. White colonists were fond of accusing King George III of being a heartless tyrant who treated them like "slaves." That stirred up uneasy feelings in the hearts and minds of at least a few, who could not reconcile condemning what King George was doing to them with the fact that they were forcing black people into perpetual servitude. Slaves seized every opportunity to point out that contradiction. Ultimately, years of bloody warfare, and then the reshaping of America once the fighting was over, had a profound impact on the black population of British North America. Neither side in the conflict had intended this to be a war to liberate a single slave. White patriots were venting their anger about the actions of a faraway government they considered arbitrary and oppressive. The British were trying to regain American loyalty. However, through the challenges they mounted to their own dire situation and through their very presence, black people helped determine the course of the Revolution and make it, at least in part, their own struggle.

Africans and African Americans were involved in the Revolutionary crisis from the beginning. Black people, a few of them free but many of them enslaved or living uneasily between slavery and freedom, participated in the various mob actions following the British government's imposition of the hated Stamp Tax in 1765. As tensions escalated, they exploited those tensions, leaving some whites apprehensive about what might happen, especially in localities where the enslaved outnumbered the white residents. For example, when a group of slaves marched through the streets of Charleston, South Carolina, the town's white Sons of Liberty were perturbed. They were unsure whether their bondsmen's cries of "Liberty! Liberty!" were simply echoing their own protests, or whether they were demanding a more complete kind of liberty for themselves.

Hundreds of miles to the north, Boston's Sons of Liberty called out mobs which included scores of black sailors. Some were free, others were slaves whose masters routinely sent them off to sea to make money. Black sailors were as incensed as white sailors about the activities of British press-gangs, who hauled seafaring men off the streets, regardless of the color of their skin, and forced them into the Royal Navy. Boston's leading white radicals gave little thought to the composition of the mob. They simply saw strength in numbers when it came to intimidating Stamp Tax agents, customs collectors and other unpopular government officials. They ignored the implications of growing black political involvement.

Generally the Boston mob was nameless and faceless—an agglomeration of people eager to display their anger over the latest move on the part of the government in London and its minions in the colonies. On occasion, however, a member of the crowd assumed a prominence that the Sons of Liberty were not prepared for. The precise role of Crispus Attucks in the events of March 5, 1770 is still open to question. Perhaps he was the prime mover in the so-called Boston Massacre, as future president John Adams, counsel for the British soldiers who stood trial for murder in the aftermath of the killings, maintained. Adams depicted Attucks as determined "to be the hero of the night."[1] Others cast him in the role of innocent bystander. Whether he was a rabble-rouser or an inquisitive passer-by cut down by panicky soldiers, one thing is certain. Attucks was a free man at the time he died because he had freed himself. Of mixed African, Indian, and most likely European ancestry, Attucks had been a slave until he had escaped from his master in Framingham, Massachusetts, two decades before the Massacre and gone to sea. He had only recently returned to the port of Boston when he heard—or inspired—the din outside the Custom House and was shot down by British troops. "The first to defy, the first to die," Attucks had a funeral worthy of a martyr for liberty.[2] A vast crowd escorted through the streets of Boston the coffins of all four of the victims of the Massacre—a fifth lingered several days before succumbing to his wounds—and buried them in a common grave.

In the tension-filled period before the actual outbreak of hostilities, other black Bostonians made white people aware of *their* commitment to liberty. Groups of slaves in and around Boston began petitioning anyone in a position of power they thought they could influence with their arguments. They pointed out the inherent injustice of slavery. They deplored the splitting up of families. They asked for land to farm and permission to work on their own account so that they could earn the money to buy their freedom. Their mention in one petition of the Spanish practice of *coartación* indicates they were well aware of the opportunities black people had elsewhere in North America to purchase themselves. One group observed to the increasingly radical Massachusetts General Court that they expected "great things" from men who were such outspoken champions of liberty.[3] Another group approached the hard-pressed royal governor, Thomas Gage, and asked for his help. Gage could take their petition as he chose—as a subtle promise of military support if he needed it or a philosophical statement of the inhumanity of chattel slavery. In the short term, neither the forces of the Crown nor their opponents heeded the petitions. When the war finally came, however, whites on both sides would have to respond to black aspirations for freedom, not only in New England but throughout the colonies.

The royal governor of Virginia, Lord Dunmore, was the first to take decisive action. In April 1775, a delegation of slaves visited Dunmore to volunteer their services as soldiers should the need arise. They knew from conversations they had overheard that a rebellion was imminent. They also knew that Dunmore had threatened to free all the slaves in Virginia if whites continued to defy his authority. In the spring Dunmore was not ready to do more than threaten and he sent the black men away. However, by the fall he had a war on his hands and he was eager to accept help from anyone who offered it. On November 7, 1775, Dunmore issued a proclamation to black slaves and white indentured servants of masters who were disloyal to His Majesty informing them that they could earn their freedom by enlisting in the regiment he was raising for King George. Dunmore outfitted his "Ethiopians" in uniforms identical to those his white troops wore, with one striking difference: the black soldiers sported sashes emblazoned with the words "Liberty to Slaves." Although Dunmore had directed his offer only to able-bodied men, entire slave families fled to join him. The royal governor seized the opportunity and assigned the black women to nursing, cooking and washing duties. However, by mid-December 1775, Dunmore had lost his land base and he and his troops withdrew to a flotilla of ships in Virginia's York River. Tragically, Dunmore's success at recruiting proved his men's undoing. In close quarters below decks in the winter of 1775–1776, smallpox ravaged his "Ethiopian" soldiers, killing hundreds who had come to him in search of freedom. Finally, in August 1776, with the military situation rapidly deteriorating in Virginia, Dunmore set sail for the loyalist stronghold of New York City.

Despite Dunmore's retreat, his use of slave troops had far-reaching repercussions. It emboldened black men fighting under his command not only to demand their freedom, but also their fair share of the military bounty. One of Dunmore's "Ethiopians," a former slave named Titus Corlies, refashioned himself in freedom as Colonel Tye. He had survived the smallpox epidemic, come north with Dunmore, and gathered his own unofficial (and interracial) band of raiders. The British military authorities respected Tye and his company, which the patriots called "banditti." They fought courageously, ostensibly on the side of King George, but always with their eyes on the prize—plunder. Again and again Tye led his men into battle, seizing prisoners and property. A courageous and charismatic free black leader like Colonel Tye, able to break through the lines of race and unite black and white fighting men, was a dangerous individual to have around. Equally dangerous were the sashes of the "Ethiopians," which proclaimed "Liberty to Slaves," implying that all slaves would receive their freedom upon a British victory. Concerned whites apparently noticed an alarming change in the behavior of their slaves. In Philadelphia, for instance, unsubstantiated reports circulated that slaves were refusing to yield the sidewalk to whites. When those white pedestrians snapped that they did not appreciate walking in the mud, the slaves responded that their day of reckoning was at hand. Philadelphia whites trembled about threats that never really existed, but whites elsewhere had good reason to worry as the war continued. Evidence of slave conspiracies surfaced in North Carolina and Georgia, undoubtedly inspired by the hope that the British would support them.

While the loyalist decision to use slaves in combat and noncombat positions undoubtedly raised the expectations of all African Americans, it also put considerable pressure on the patriots, who had initially opposed black military service. On July 2, 1775, when George Washington arrived in Cambridge, Massachusetts to assume command of the Continental Army, he was shocked to see musket-toting black men mixing with white volunteers. Washington knew that the Continental Congress did not want any black men in the new fighting force, but he could see with his own eyes that they were there. Some were slaves who served in place of their masters or whose masters had given them permission to serve. Many were runaways who presented themselves to recruiters as free men, and those recruiters wisely did not ask questions about their status. Others were free and had chosen to enlist because they truly believed in the cause of independence or were motivated by the bounties of cash or land that different communities were offering to get recruits. A good many, like Salem Poor, Barzillai Lew, and Peter Salem, had already distinguished themselves in the early encounters with the British. The army needed them, and it did not seem right to reward them for their courage under fire by sending them away.

Nonetheless, Washington hesitated, and so did his fellow officers. Perhaps they could allow those who were free to serve. Perhaps they could permit those who had already joined up to reenlist but not accept any new black recruits. Finally, in the early weeks of 1776, Congress took the decision out of the hands of the military men by rendering what they intended would be their final ruling: there was no room in the army for black soldiers, free or enslaved. The individual colonies, most of them in the midst of declaring themselves independent states, by and large endorsed the ban on black enlistment. This was a white man's war. If black people hoped to use it to win their freedom, they would have to think again.

However, since the British actively recruited black men, white patriots ultimately had to reconsider their own ban on black enlistment. Within a year after the Continental Congress excluded African Americans from military service, George Washington himself had become far less squeamish about allowing black troops into his army. He was confronting a grave manpower shortage, and he was prepared to cope with it as best he could. On January 2, 1777, driven by military necessity, the Continental Army issued an order allowing freemen to enlist. The recruitment of slaves to serve, however, would take another two years. In March 1779, after many months of nagging by Washington and his fellow commanders, who were contending with desertions, an ever-lengthening casualty list, and a shortage of white volunteers, the Continental Congress reversed its earlier ban and approved the use of slaves. In essence, the delegates were recognizing what was already happening. One by one, the newly independent states in the North and the Upper South were loosening their own prohibitions on the enlistment of black men.

Rhode Island went the furthest when it came to arming slaves, and it did so because it had no alternative. By 1778, much of the state was under British control, and lawmakers concluded that they could only meet their quota of men for the Continental Army by authorizing the state to purchase slaves from their owners and muster them into service into the First Rhode Island Regiment, later nicknamed the "Black Regiment." The decision to compensate slaveholders and then arm the slaves after promising them their liberty was a bold move in a state where slavery was both socially and economically important. The authorities recognized that they would have to tie enlistment to emancipation. Any fighting man equipped with a gun would turn it on his oppressors, or at the very least desert to the enemy, if he knew that he had to return to slavery once the war was over.

Massachusetts lawmakers looked at Rhode Island's Black Regiment and contemplated a similar move. Although they eventually decided not to follow Rhode Island's lead, they did lift their earlier ban on black men serving in the military, and a good many did so. Some found their way into an all-black company known as the Bucks of America. Many, though, served in what were basically integrated units.

Maryland was the only Southern state that specifically allowed slaves to enlist. It also made free men of color as well as white men subject to the draft. Virginia took a more conservative approach, as did Delaware and North Carolina, ruling that free black men could serve, but slaves could only do so as substitutes for their masters. When it emerged after the war that some white men had sent their slaves off to the front lines and then reneged on their promise to free them, Virginia lawmakers were disgusted. They insisted that any slave who could demonstrate that he had fought in place of his master on the understanding that he would get his freedom would indeed get it. Of course, furnishing proof of a promise of freedom was no easy matter if master and slave had had merely a verbal agreement.

The situation in South Carolina and Georgia was very different indeed from that in the Upper South. In 1779, with the British achieving one victory after another in the Lower South, and gathering hordes of black recruits, the Continental Congress demanded action. Delegates had long since reversed themselves on the matter of allowing black men into the Continental Army. Now they took an even more radical stance. South Carolinians must consent to the creation of one or more black regiments. The state needed to muster at least 3,000 black men without further delay. It went without saying that South Carolina would have to draw most of those men from its slave population, and obviously the authorities would need to guarantee the black soldiers their freedom. This initiative on the part of the Continental Congress was not about the morality or immorality of slavery: it was about victory or defeat.

The members of South Carolina's planter elite threw up their hands in horror. Slaves outnumbered whites in the state, and that made them feel very vulnerable. They pointed to past episodes of racial unrest. The slaves were constantly plotting, sometimes with the help of free black relatives and friends. If the Continental Congress forced South Carolina's slave owners to emancipate and arm their slaves, there would be an orgy of violence.

Black men would go on the rampage. They would not fight the British. They would kill their masters instead. Lawmakers announced that rather than accede to the demands of Congress they would pull out of the war effort. Georgia's leaders announced that they would follow suit. Black men, enslaved and free, in the Lower South *did* serve in the Revolution, but with some notable exceptions they did so on the British side.

And after June 1779, there was even more reason for black men to do so. On June 30, royal Commander-in-Chief Sir Henry Clinton, realizing that the military use of African Americans could play a decisive role in winning the war, announced that it was official British policy to liberate any slave who made it to British lines. Seeking their freedom, thousands of slaves flocked to the loyalists, who used them in arms as well as in various noncombat posts. In several cities, including Philadelphia and New York, the British organized companies of Black Pioneers to do everything from guarding prisoners to keeping the streets clean. In the North and the South black recruits foraged, spied, drove wagons, and served as personal attendants to British officers.

In addition to participating in the land-based conflict, black men took part in many naval actions. Tough and dangerous though life in the navy might be, it was as good a means of gaining one's liberty as enlisting in the army, and the prospect of plunder appealed just as strongly to black men as it did to white men. Fugitive slaves, especially those with seafaring experience, joined the Royal Navy in search of freedom. Other fugitives, along with hundreds of black men who were legally free, joined the Continental Navy. Almost all of the newly independent states created their own navies and each faced the same problem—getting enough experienced men and boys to crew their vessels. Free blacks volunteered because they believed in the patriot cause or because they understood that sea service generally meant equal pay for equal work. The enslaved looked for captains they thought might not inquire into the legal status of any sturdy-looking man who was eager to serve. Again and again slave owners lamented that valuable "property" had run away and headed to the closest seaport. Recapturing a slave who had gone to sea was far more challenging than retaking that same individual while he was still on dry land, and if he survived he was obviously going to make sure he did not return to his "home" port.

In addition to those who served in the Continental Navy or the state navies, thousands of other seafarers, black and white, opted to become privateers. As the war progressed, merchants and ship owners followed the venerable tradition established by the British and the French in earlier conflicts. Under license from their home state or from the newly-organized United States, they refitted trading vessels as armed raiders with the goal of plundering enemy shipping—and everyone, from the captain and the owner of the privateer down to the humblest ship's boy, got a share of the plunder. With money at stake, captains of privateers did not care about the race or the status of a crew member. Black men and boys thronged the wharves, eager to ship out, make money, and in the case of runaway slaves make good their escape.

After the British surrender at Yorktown in 1781, as British commanders began preparing to evacuate their forces from the ports they still held, the ex-slaves who had escaped and joined the British feared they would be left behind. They grew even more desperate when they learned that the peace treaty that officially ended hostilities stipulated that slaves must be returned to their owners. They crowded on to British ships, pleading to go somewhere—anywhere—where they could be free. Sometimes they met with a sympathetic hearing. Realizing what was going on, George Washington raced to New York and insisted to the British commander, Sir Guy Carleton, that the terms of surrender required him to hand over all the runaways who were within British lines. Carleton refused, maintaining that the British had made a pledge of freedom to the slaves who sided with them and he intended to honor that pledge.

At least 10,000 black people, and perhaps as many as 20,000, left with the British. For some it was only a brief respite. British officers who were far less honorable than Carleton re-enslaved them. Other black loyalists were more fortunate. Hundreds headed to England and tried to build new lives for themselves there. Many more went to the West Indies where they resettled as free people, although maintaining one's liberty in the midst of a slave-holding society was fraught with difficulties. By far the largest contingent found a dubious freedom in Nova Scotia. The failure of the British authorities to provide for them as generously as they provided for white loyalists prompted the black loyalists to petition the government in London for relief, and led to a mass exodus to Britain's new West African colony of Sierra Leone. However, enough black Americans remained in Nova Scotia to establish their own communities, some of which survive to this day. Few black loyalists received pensions because the British government considered it payment enough that they were no longer slaves. A black man needed to prove that he had been free before the war to have any hope of getting a penny for his services to the king.

On the patriot side, some black men returned from the battlefield only to have their masters on whose behalf they had fought reclaim them as slaves. Others came back to enjoy their freedom, and in some instances with enough money to buy their loved ones out of bondage. They returned with tales to tell, and with valuable military or naval experience. In most instances, they had fought alongside white men. Ironically, few black men who had fought in the Revolution had done so in all-black units. Not until the Korean War would the United States have such a racially integrated fighting force.

Black veterans had often traveled far from home. They had met people from many different backgrounds and they had endured all kinds of hardships—hunger, exposure to the elements, inadequate clothing, and harsh discipline, along with separation from friends and family. For the majority, whether they had been free before they enlisted or whether they had been enslaved, these were hardships with which they were already painfully familiar. The home front to which these men returned was very different from the one they had left. The war and their role in it had led to a period of profound change for themselves, their families, the entire black population, and the nation as a whole. For some black people the war and its aftermath meant freedom and the chance to achieve a measure of social and economic independence. For others it saw the betrayal of a dream.

The war for black liberty would continue long after the British surrender and long after the thirteen newly independent states had united to form a new nation. Nonetheless, the American Revolution had an important impact on slavery. Prior to the Revolution, slavery existed in all of the British colonies of North America. During and after the Revolution, many of the newly emerging states in the North took steps to end the system, either by abolishing slavery in their state constitutions or by adopting gradual abolition laws.

Vermont was the first state to outlaw slavery in its state constitution. The fact that slavery had historically played a minor role in Vermont meant there were few black people in the state. White Vermonters did not anticipate a difficult transition from slavery to freedom when they framed a constitution in 1777 that declared that "No male person ought . . . to serve any person as a servant, slave, or apprentice after he arrives to the age of twenty-one years, nor female in like manner after . . . the age of eighteen years."[4] As for civil rights for free people of African ancestry, lawmakers left things vague, but apparently black men could and did vote in Vermont.

Pennsylvania's Gradual Abolition Law was the culmination of decades of antislavery agitation by black people, both enslaved and free, and by white critics of slavery. Although the Quakers had rid themselves of slave-holding, most of their neighbors had not. Pressuring Pennsylvania to live up to the principles of liberty was an uphill battle. The Pennsylvania Society for Promoting the Abolition of Slavery, the Relief of Free Negroes Unlawfully Held in Bondage, and for Improving the Condition of the African

Race, composed largely of Quakers, disintegrated during the war, although it was reborn a few years later. Black Pennsylvanians cooperated with white abolitionists, but they did not rely on their efforts alone. Slaves did everything they could to gain their own freedom, while the free helped their enslaved friends and family members and endeavored to improve their own situation.

In 1780, with the war still raging, Pennsylvania lawmakers finally approved a gradual abolition law. The law was limited in scope, and applied only to children born after the date of its passage (March 1), and then only when they reached the age of twenty-eight. Until then they were to be bound or "apprenticed" to the people who owned their mothers: they could be sold, leased, even left with real estate and farm animals in people's wills. And, given life expectancy at the time, they might well die before they ever secured their full freedom. Although Pennsylvania had taken its first wavering steps toward ending human bondage, the law said nothing about what rights free people of color would enjoy. It would be left to black women and men themselves to give true meaning to their freedom, and they would prove resolute in their determination to make sure that they and their descendants were free in more than name only.

The path to ending slavery in Massachusetts was a tortuous one. Within the white community the debate over the ownership of one human being by another had gone on for decades, although few whites were willing to do more than pay lip service to the notion of liberty for all. Black people did not leave it to a handful of well-disposed whites to act for them. They pushed the issue beyond platitudes and high-sounding but empty phrases. In 1780, the newly independent state had adopted a constitution that said that "all men are born free and equal." Two slaves, Quock Walker and Mumbet *alias* Elizabeth Freeman, brought separate court actions in which they and their lawyers cited that "free and equal" clause and tested its deeper meaning. The attorneys for Walker and Freeman contended that unless anyone could prove that the term "all men" did not apply to black people, the constitution effectively outlawed slavery. While Walker and Freeman gained *their* freedom, it was a matter of opinion whether slavery in Massachusetts was illegal. In the 1783 Walker case Chief Justice William Cushing ruled that "the idea of slavery is inconsistent with our own conduct and Constitution."[5] However, lawmakers did not follow up on the Walker and Freeman verdicts by introducing an abolition law. Individual slaves took matters into their own hands by pressuring their owners to liberate them or by simply walking away. Some owners stubbornly insisted that the law still protected their property rights, and some black people remained in bondage for years, but by the late 1780s it was clear that the institution of slavery was dying in Massachusetts.

New Hampshire took as long and as twisted a path to abolition as did Massachusetts, and it, too, left the question of black rights vague and ill-defined. If the Granite State did not have as many slaves as Massachusetts, it still had a substantial number, and they were assertive and articulate. In 1779, slaves in and around Portsmouth seized the initiative, possibly with help from members of the admittedly small free community of color. They approached the legislature and challenged lawmakers to live up to the ideals of independence and rights for all. They wanted to be treated like other inhabitants and have "an Opportunity of evincing to the World our Love of Freedom by . . . opposing the Efforts of Tyranny and Oppression over the Country in which we ourselves have been so long injuriously enslaved." If New Hampshire abolished slavery—a practice that flew in the face of "Justice and Humanity"—they pledged that every black man would be happy to fight alongside his white brothers against the forces of the King of England.[6] In 1783, the state adopted a constitution that said that "all men [were] born equal and independent," and had certain "natural rights," which included "enjoying . . . life and liberty."[7] That did not amount to immediate emancipation, but the enslaved claimed their freedom from owners who were not sure they could hold on to them. Within a decade slavery had faded away. What did not fade so completely were old patterns of thought on the part of white people in New Hampshire. Black people determined to enjoy the same rights as their white neighbors now that they were free faced many challenges.

Emancipation was also a long time coming in Rhode Island, the smallest state in the Union. Despite pressure from the slaves themselves, from the small but vocal free community of color, which included proud veterans of the Rhode Island Black Regiment, and from white sympathizers, slavery had powerful supporters. In 1784, though, the state legislature finally passed an abolition bill. Like the Pennsylvania law, the Rhode Island law only gradually phased out slavery. Children born to enslaved women after March 1, 1784 would eventually be free—females at eighteen and males at twenty-one. Until then they had to serve whoever owned their mothers. Once a black Rhode Islander ceased to be a slave, that did not mean he or she could settle down and live as white people did. Rhode Island had long since adopted the same tactic as Massachusetts when it came to dealing with anyone who seemed likely to become a public charge. The authorities "warned out" or expelled that individual, and if necessary their entire family. Liberated into a harsh world with few job opportunities and even fewer resources, African

Americans often gravitated to the lower rungs of society, and that made them subject to the full weight of the law. They could be driven out of the township in which they lived, or forced over the state line into an equally unfriendly setting in Massachusetts or Connecticut.

Despite the large number of slaves in Connecticut, the antislavery forces eventually prevailed there. Children born to enslaved women after March 1, 1784—the same date as in Rhode Island—would become free when they reached adulthood. Connecticut's abolition law did nothing for those born before its passage. Theoretically, they would remain enslaved for the rest of their lives. As had happened in other states, though, some slaveholders released their slaves, while hundreds of bondspeople simply absconded. Judging by newspaper advertisements for runaways, Connecticut's slaves were both resourceful and determined. If the law would not grant them their freedom, they would take it.

Across the North in the 1770s and 1780s black people existed in freedom, in slavery, and in an uncertain position midway between slavery and freedom, with an end to their bondage in sight but with precious little freedom in their immediate future. Only Vermont had abolished slavery outright. Most Northern states had adopted gradual abolition, and although lawmakers in New Jersey and New York had debated abolition on a number of occasions, they had yet to take decisive action. And in none of the Northern states did the courts or the legislatures declare free black people citizens. Although they might not be slaves, they were somehow less than equal to whites in the eyes of the law and in the minds of their white neighbors. In 1788, for example, the Massachusetts General Court barred from the state all "Rogues, vagabonds, common beggars, and other idle, disorderly, and lewd Persons."[8] Not surprisingly, whites thought that many free blacks belonged to one of those unwelcome and unwanted groups. Expulsion of the black poor, the binding out of their children, and the routine incarceration of black lawbreakers for longer terms than those that white lawbreakers received for the same offense—these practices were commonplace throughout the North. The states retained their old colonial-era restrictions and added new ones whenever lawmakers concluded that the free black population was getting too troublesome.

In the immediate post-Revolutionary period the South was anything but united on the issue of black freedom. As they had done in the colonial era, slave owners in South Carolina and Georgia generally emancipated those individuals to whom they had a personal connection, including their con-cubines, their children, their biracial half-siblings, and their favored house slaves. The result was a small community of light-skinned people whose ties to their emancipators often endured into freedom. By contrast, in the Upper South emancipations were more general, and they took place for reasons of ideological or religious commitment, or as a result of economic consider-ations. And of course the slaves themselves pushed hard. To imply that they sat back and waited for whites to liberate them is to ignore a vital part of the picture.

The enslaved seized their freedom through flight. They also sued, claiming that they were the descendants of white women. After a couple of well-publicized court victories in the 1780s, hundreds of slaves all over Maryland suddenly "discovered" that they had white female ancestors. When light-skinned slaves hinted that they had befriended a lawyer who would see justice done, some masters actually bargained with those slaves: if there was no more talk about white grandmothers and great-grandmothers and if they served quietly for a few more years they would get their freedom. It was not a game for the faint-of-heart. The power obviously lay with the master, but there was just a chance that he might want to avoid an expensive court case.

With or without the threat of lawsuits, other slaves gained their freedom. The Upper South was wavering. Tobacco prices tumbled in the 1780s as planters discovered that they had lost their once-reliable overseas customers. Instead of tobacco, they turned to growing wheat and raising hogs, only to find that they did not need as big a labor force. They could not sell their excess slaves because the market was glutted and no one was buying, so in some instances they let those slaves earn the price of their freedom. It also became simpler and cheaper to liberate one's slaves. In 1782, Virginia rewrote its law to allow owners to free almost anyone under the age of forty-five. Delaware and Maryland also eased the restrictions on freedom. Owners could essentially do what they liked with their "property." Some called in their lawyers and instructed them to draw up formal deeds of eman-cipation. Others simply told their slaves they did not want or need them any longer. The free population received an additional boost as a result of African-American enlistment during the war. Black men who had served in their masters' stead pressed hard to make sure that their service did indeed translate into freedom. The region was also still feeling the reverberations from the Great Awakening. Some whites could not square slave ownership with their religious principles. For other owners the motivation was not so much evangelical religion as devotion to the libertarian principles of the Revolution.

In sharp contrast to the Upper South, the Lower South was largely untouched by religious or philosophical impulses to end slavery. The political leaders of South Carolina and Georgia had made their views abundantly clear when they had refused to liberate their slaves to fight the British. Once the war was over, they were determined to maintain their control over their remaining slaves. The legislatures of the two states made a few minor concessions to owners who wanted to emancipate one or two favored slaves, but they soon clamped down. Although the economy was no better in the Lower South in the 1780s than it was in the Upper South, slave owners remained firmly committed to the notion that slavery was the natural condition of black people. They also reflected on the fact that whites were in the minority across the region. If they freed their slaves, they feared that black people would take over. They might avenge their sufferings or they might intermarry with whites. Both prospects filled white Georgians and South Carolinians with dread. They did as they had always done. They liberated enslaved people to whom they had ties of blood and affection and did their best to keep the rest in bondage. The free black population did grow in the immediate postwar years as people maneuvered their way out of slavery, formed stable family units and had children who were born free. However, in comparison to the Upper South, where thousands of slaves gained their liberty every year during the 1780s, the free population of the Lower South grew at a very slow rate

At the national level, liberty for black people proved such a sensitive issue that white politicians backed away from dealing with it. Thomas Jefferson's first draft of the Declaration of Independence had included a stinging denunciation of King George III for, among other evidence of his wickedness, making war on the peoples of Africa, enslaving them, and dumping them in the American colonies. Many of Jefferson's fellow delegates to the Continental Congress found his words unsettling. They reasoned, not surprisingly, that if they accepted his draft and did ultimately prevail against the armies of Great Britain, they had committed themselves to doing away with slavery. The offending passage disappeared. However, even in its modified form, the Declaration's resounding phrases about "all men" being created equal and being entitled to life, liberty and the pursuit of happiness heartened black people who heard them or read them. On July 8, 1776, when the High Sheriff of Philadelphia read the Declaration to the populace for the first time, a nine-year-old black child stood in the crowd in the State House Yard and listened intently. The promises enshrined in the document that the Continental Congress had approved four days earlier resonated with James Forten and would continue to do so. As soon as he was old enough, he signed up aboard a patriot privateer. He was captured by the British, rejected a tempting offer to switch sides, and endured months of captivity on a prison-ship. He believed wholeheartedly that the new nation was worth risking his life for. Thomas Jefferson and his brethren had spoken so eloquently about freedom. They could hardly continue to hold their fellow Americans in slavery. Forten himself was freeborn, although he sympathized with the enslaved and wanted to see their bondage ended. Equally important to him was the "pursuit of happiness." He concluded that meant full citizenship for everyone once slavery had been banished from American soil. As the years passed and Forten grew to manhood, he discovered that America was only partially fulfilling its commitment to liberty and justice for all.

The Articles of Confederation, the framework of government the delegates to the Continental Congress formally adopted in 1781, said nothing about slavery, emancipation, or rights for black people. Those were matters for the individual states to decide upon. There was one piece of legislation passed during the period of Confederation, however, that had far-reaching implications for the nation as a whole and most especially for black Americans. The Northwest Ordinance of 1787 described in detail what was to happen to the land between the Ohio and Mississippi Rivers and the Great Lakes, the old Illinois Country. The United States had gained the territory from Britain at the end of the war. Lawmakers proposed to divide the vast area into five territories, each of which could apply for statehood. None of those states could permit slavery to exist within their borders. Few of the congressmen who approved the Ordinance were ardent abolitionists. Their goal was to keep the Old Northwest for white family farmers by barring entry to planters from the South with huge gangs of slaves. The fate of the slaves who were already living in the Old Northwest, some of them from the days when the French had controlled the region, remained uncertain. The governments of the new states—states that did not even exist yet—would ultimately have to address that thorny question, along with the issue of what rights, if any, free black people would have.

When the Founding Fathers gathered in Philadelphia in 1787 to revise the Articles of Confederation, and ended by crafting an entirely new document, they again skirted around the matter of slavery. They discovered how volatile it could be when they tackled the apportioning of political representation. While each state would have two senators, its number of representatives would depend on the size of its population. Determining who could vote was left up to each state, but determining who should be counted was another matter. The Three-Fifths Compromise resolved the impasse by proposing that, in reckoning population, five slaves would be equal to three nonslaves. So much for the slaves, but when it came to black people who were not enslaved, the Founding Fathers said nothing, beyond implying that the census-takers would enumerate them with all other free people.

As the white Founding Fathers put the finishing touches to the U.S. Constitution and prepared to depart Philadelphia, a group of free black Founding Fathers set to work. They were a diverse group—Richard Allen, a self-purchased ex-slave from Delaware; Absalom Jones, another former slave who had paid for his freedom and become a moderately successful craftsman; William Gray, an independent tradesman; and some two dozen other men, all of them free and all of them determined to use their freedom well. Their immediate goal was to create an organization that would secure their own and their families' futures. They knew that if they fell upon hard times they could not expect help from the white community, so they undertook to pay money into a common fund on which they could draw in time of need. Their mutual benefit society was not the only one in existence. Free blacks in Newport, Rhode Island had already formed the Newport African Union, and there were probably similar societies in other cities and towns. However, the Free African Society was undoubtedly the largest and most ambitious of any of the groups. In part, that was because of the sheer size of Philadelphia's free community of color, which numbered around 1,800 people in 1787, more than any other city in the former British colonies. The message that Jones, Allen, Gray and the other officers of the new Free African Society wanted to send to whites and blacks, though, was about more than strength in numbers. They pledged themselves to live lives that were beyond reproach, and they called upon other free people of color to subscribe to the same moral values of thrift and piety, temperance, charity, neighborliness, faithfulness, and respect for authority because adhering to those values would benefit them all, and because it would prove to doubting whites that all black people, in Philadelphia and throughout the nation, deserved freedom and equal treatment.

Allen, Jones, Gray and their friends answered loudly and clearly one fundamental question, namely whether they believed that black people had a future in America, or at least anywhere in the vicinity of white people. The issue had already surfaced in the petitions that the slaves in Massachusetts had sent to the General Court and to the British governor in the months preceding the Revolution. Some of the petitioners had declared that if they got their freedom they would leave for Africa, while others had spoken of moving to the western fringes of Massachusetts. Perhaps these two groups of black men had reasoned that whites would be more apt to liberate them if they promised to go away, or perhaps they thought they would be truly free only when they could live as *they* chose, not as whites chose for them.

The men of the Free African Society engaged in that debate head-on. Heartened by Britain's creation of the colony of Sierra Leone as a refuge for black loyalists, and disheartened by their own "calamitous state" in America, the men in the Newport African Union contemplated relocating to Africa and asked the Philadelphians what they thought. The Philadelphians wished them well, but they rejected the notion of emigration. They planned on staying in America.[9]

While they regretted that many whites were choosing to ignore the nation's founding principles of "life, liberty and the pursuit of happiness" for all Americans, the men of the Free African Society, the leaders of the largest community of free people in the United States, voiced confidence that better times lay ahead. They had been born in America. Some of them had fought for its independence. They *belonged* in America just as white people did. One's ancestry was immaterial. Birth and loyalty and commitment were what mattered. They had no intention of leaving. They were worthy citizens of the new nation, as worthy as white Americans. They would stay and see the promise of the Revolution fulfilled.

CHAPTER THREE

~

Race, Liberty, and Citizenship in the New Nation, 1790–1820

In 1790, the United States conducted its first census. An army of enumerators trudged or rode on horseback across sixteen states and territories, collected their data, and tabulated the results. They put the total U.S. population at just under four million. Black people accounted for over 757,000, or about one in five Americans. Of that number, less than 8 percent were free. By 1820, the nation and its people were very different. The United States now comprised 27 states and territories and its population was over 9.5 million, a figure that included more than 1.5 million slaves and well over a quarter of a million free blacks. By this point, more than 13 percent of the black population was free.

Within those totals and percentages there were huge regional disparities. More free blacks lived in the slave states of the South than in the Northern "free" states. However, in some Southern states the number of free people

Table 3.1   United States Population, 1790–1860

Year	Total Population	Slaves	Free Blacks
1790	3,929,827	697,897	59,466
1800	5,305,925	893,041	108,395
1810	7,239,814	1,191,364	186,446
1820	9,638,191	1,538,038	233,504
1830	12,866,020	2,009,043	319,599
1840	17,069,453	2,487,043	386,303
1850	23,191,876	3,204,313	434,495
1860	31,443,321	3,953,760	487,970

Source: Federal Population Schedules for the Years 1790 through 1860

was very small. In 1790, as many free blacks lived in the city of Philadelphia as lived in the entire state of South Carolina. Two states in the Upper South, Maryland and Virginia, accounted for almost 21,000 of the nation's 59,500 free people. By 1820, the demographic patterns were even more marked. The Lower South had slightly more than 20,000 "free colored" residents, but over half of them lived in just one state, Louisiana. Georgia's free black population was on a par with that of Boston. As was the case with the American population as a whole, free blacks were more likely to dwell in rural areas than in towns and cities, but the growth of the urban black population was very significant. New York City's free black community surged from just over a thousand individuals in 1790 to 10,500 by 1820, Philadelphia's went from 1,800 to 10,710, and, most spectacularly of all, Baltimore's leaped from 323 to 10,326—a massive increase in just one generation. In Baltimore, a city in the slave South, more black people were free than were enslaved.

Though freedom came to some black people, the majority of black Americans lived in slavery. The number of free people rose nationwide, but so, too, did the number of slaves. In some states slavery was dead or dying. In others it was thriving, and showing every sign of continuing to do so. In the United States as a whole, the prevailing condition of people of African birth or descent was lifelong servitude, not liberty, and certainly not equality.

Demographics are important in understanding the patterns of freedom and slavery that evolved in the generation after Independence, but it is equally important to look beyond the check marks on the census-takers' tally sheets to see what the numbers tell us about the life of the nation and about individual lives. This is the story of black people securing their freedom, passing that freedom on to their children, and forging new communities based on the principles of liberty and opportunity over the course of three tumultuous decades. It is also the story of the nation as it extended its geographic boundaries and grappled with the issues of freedom, race, and the meaning of "citizenship."

Scarcely had the census takers completed work on the first census than a wave of immigrants from Haiti pushed upward the total of free blacks. Their arrival had implications that went far beyond mere statistics. In 1791, the slaves in the French Caribbean colony of Saint Domingue, today's nation of Haiti, rose up under the leadership of the charismatic Toussaint L'Ouverture. The slaughter that ensued as they fought for their liberty and their masters tried to force them back into bondage was truly terrible. White Americans heard of the atrocities and were appalled at the thought that the "contagion of liberty," as some called it, might spread to America's shores. The responses of black Americans were more complex. While many took heart from the destruction of Saint Domingue's brutal slave system, spokesmen for the emerging free black communities in the North and Upper South hastened to reassure whites that they would never sanction violence on the part of their own friends and family members who were still enslaved and that the United States could easily avert a bloodbath by abolishing slavery and recognizing black people as citizens. What was happening in the West Indies need not, and hopefully would not, happen on American soil.

The killings on Saint Domingue continued. The rebels made no distinction between their oppressors based upon race, and on Saint Domingue there were both white and "free colored" slaveholders. The *gens de couleur libres*, the mixed-race descendants of French men and African women, had as much to fear as white planters, and they joined them in fleeing to safety in North America. Once in the United States, the white exiles received sympathy and even charitable assistance, since many of them had escaped with little more than the clothes on their backs. The mixed-race newcomers received neither sympathy nor charity. Whites in the United States found the presence of the so-called "French Negroes" very worrying. They did not understand that these free people had actually supported slavery. They persisted in seeing *them* as rebels, as threatening in their way as the forces of Toussaint L'Ouverture. The *gens de couleur libres* were so different from American free blacks—in religion and language and in their sense of themselves. On Saint Domingue they had constituted a separate caste midway between the white planter elite and the slaves, and they had enjoyed certain privileges as a result. Once they set foot in the United States, however, they discovered that their privileges vanished. Whites treated them just as contemptuously as they did American free blacks. Some of the lighter-skinned *gens de couleur* responded by "passing" as white. Some kept to themselves and tried to maintain a separate identity as French-speaking "colored" Catholics. A good many, though, realized that they had no alternative but to ally with American-born free people of color. They forged friendships with them, intermarried with them, and ultimately increased by their presence not only the numbers of free people but the cultural diversity of the free community of color.

Although a few of the Saint Dominguan exiles headed to New England, most ventured no further north than New York City. New England's free black population grew not because of the arrival of immigrants from the Caribbean but because the states in the region had done away with slavery. Abolishing slavery did not mean abandoning the patterns of thought and behavior that had governed the interactions between blacks and whites for generations. Freedom had not come with much in the way of rights. In Massachusetts, New Hampshire, and Vermont—and for a time in

Rhode Island and Connecticut—black men could vote, and they made use of that, supporting any candidate they thought would address their concerns, although they learned quickly that politicians had a habit of repudiating campaign promises once they got into office. Even with the chance to participate in the political process, black New Englanders received constant reminders of their second-class status. In 1800, the authorities in Boston expelled 239 out-of-state black people, and there were no doubt similar less well publicized "warnings out" elsewhere. Across the region, many of the repressive colonial-era laws remained in place.

The situation in the Mid-Atlantic states with respect to black freedom was more complicated. Pennsylvania had enacted gradual emancipation during the Revolution, and each year more black people became free. Not surprisingly, blacks from other states flocked to Pennsylvania, and especially to the city of Philadelphia, in search of work and a place of refuge. Some were free, while others were runaway slaves. Whites complained incessantly that the census figures underreported the numbers of black residents of Philadelphia and the surrounding counties because many hid from the census-takers. The 1793 federal Fugitive Slave Law gave them every reason to lie low. The law empowered slave owners and professional slave catchers to cross state lines in search of runaways. In an era before fingerprints and photographs, vague written descriptions sufficed as proof of identity, and the description of one black person could easily fit another of approximately the same age, height, and build. Slave catchers picked up people and hustled them before a magistrate who made an on-the-spot determination as to whether or not they were in fact escaped slaves. In Pennsylvania and throughout the Mid-Atlantic region, free people needed to be constantly on their guard. The enduring legacy of slavery robbed them of any real sense of security.

Pennsylvania had acted in 1780 to phase out slavery. New York took much longer to begin the process. The forces of antislavery, black and white, achieved a partial victory in the legislature in 1799 with the passage of a law that provided for the freeing of children born to enslaved women after July 4 of that year, although not until they were in their twenties. In 1817, lawmakers finally decreed that on July 4, 1827 slavery in New York would officially end and all the remaining slaves in the state would be free.

Long before the state of New York abolished slavery, New York City had an articulate and well-organized free black community. There were also sizable clusters of free people in other urban centers. Lawmakers might envision African Americans as a permanent underclass, even after emancipation, but that was not the future black New Yorkers accepted for themselves. They wanted what they considered their birthright, namely equality and full citizenship. Affluent free black men were legally entitled to vote in New York, and members of New York City's small but rapidly growing entrepreneurial elite were particularly active in that regard. They favored Alexander Hamilton's Federalists, who were usually antislavery in their sympathies. When Democrats attacked them as mindless tools of the opposition, black New Yorkers responded that they had enough sense to vote for the party that guaranteed them "the blessings of Liberty and Justice."[1]

New Jersey took longer than New York to start dismantling the institution of slavery. Not until 1804 did that state pass a gradual abolition law—and it was very gradual. Well into the 1830s, New Jersey had more slaves than any other Northern state, and black freedom was almost a contradiction in terms because the state continued to impose so many limitations on what African Americans could and could not do. However, in freedom as in slavery, black residents of New Jersey banded together, determined not to be marginalized politically or economically.

By 1805, every one of the Northern states had set slavery on the path to extinction. That did not mean that in any of those states black people could expect the same treatment as whites. Dissatisfied though black Northerners were with half-measures, few would have disputed that even limited freedom was preferable to enslavement. Individually and collectively, they struggled to move beyond the lowly status that so many whites thought should be theirs in perpetuity, even when they ceased to be slaves. Black people in the South were equally determined, although the challenges they faced were much greater.

If slavery was dying in the North, it was getting a new lease on life in the South. However, the South was not a single entity. In terms of population, economy, and ideology, the Upper and the Lower South were very different, and for several decades it seemed possible that freedom would become the norm for black people in Virginia and the surrounding states, even as South Carolina and Georgia clung tenaciously to the institution of slavery. Numbers alone suggest that the Upper South was committed to emancipation. But if the number of free people was rising, so was the number of slaves. Even so, the three decades following the Revolution witnessed a dramatic transformation of free black life in the Upper South. Free communities emerged in localities where none had existed previously. People struggled to make a living for themselves and their families. They organized churches and schools and self-improvement societies. Above all, they made it clear to their white neighbors that they would do whatever they needed to do to safeguard their own freedom and help other black Southerners extricate themselves from bondage.

In the immediate post-Independence years tens of thousands of slaves in Maryland, Virginia, North Carolina, and Delaware had gained their freedom. Slave owners had responded to a number of imperatives, from religious impulses to the Revolutionary rhetoric of liberty for all, from the need for black troops to fight the British to the economic upheavals that made slavery less profitable than it had been. By the 1790s, however, things were changing. Religious denominations like the Baptists and the Methodists that had once denounced slavery were back-pedaling, and prices for slaves in the expanding Cotton Kingdom in the Lower South were rising. If an owner in Virginia or North Carolina did not have enough work for all of his slaves, he could sell them to a trader. He need not set them free.

Throughout the Upper South, emancipations declined and restrictions on free people intensified as whites began to feel uneasy when they realized just how large a segment of the black population was in fact free. The various state legislatures crafted laws to make securing one's liberty more difficult. No longer was it sufficient for an owner simply to decide to free a slave. New regulations obliged masters and mistresses to prove in court that a slave had earned his or her freedom through "meritorious service." Some courts interpreted that very loosely, while others routinely turned down all requests to approve manumissions. After 1806, Virginia required all newly-freed slaves to leave the state. Some managed to secure waivers from the courts. Those who did not have any influential white friends to intercede for them simply stayed put and hoped to avoid detection. Other states throughout the region adopted similar exclusion laws, since they did not want hundreds of ex-slaves from Virginia crossing over *their* borders and taking up residence.

Ironically, for a brief moment white Virginians had debated the wisdom of wholesale emancipation. In 1800, they had been horrified to learn that a trusted slave craftsman, Gabriel, had been planning a massive rebellion. It reminded them all too vividly of what had happened on Saint Domingue. They executed Gabriel and all of his co-conspirators and then began asking what they could do to prevent future insurrections. A few bold souls maintained that the wisest course would be to give the slaves what they wanted, namely their liberty. That prompted questions about what the racial landscape would look like in Virginia if slavery ceased to exist. Few whites were willing to live alongside free black people as equals. They silenced the antislavery radicals. Instead of emancipation they demanded harsher punishments for any acts of disobedience on the part of the slaves and tighter controls on free blacks to limit their abilities to conspire with the slaves.

Although the laws became more restrictive, the free community of color in the Upper South kept growing. It grew as the region itself grew. Kentucky and Tennessee joined the Union in the 1790s. Both entered as slave states and both patterned their laws on those of the older states, Tennessee on the North Carolina code and Kentucky on that of Virginia. Neither Kentucky nor Tennessee wanted to encourage free black settlers, but the repressive laws could not keep black people out of the new states. They were as eager as white people to lay claim to good farmland or, if they had skilled trades, to seek employment in the fledgling townships of Lexington, Louisville, and Nashville.

In both the older and the newer states of the Upper South the free black population continued to grow as free couples formed stable family units and had children, as owners turned their slaves loose without bothering with the formalities, and as runaways quietly blended in among those who were legally free. For the Upper South's free people of color, life was full of contradictions. Their sheer numbers gave them opportunities to organize, to develop community institutions, and to try to build secure futures, even as their assertiveness and their very presence perturbed their white neighbors.

The situation in the Lower South was strikingly different. Georgia and South Carolina proved as hostile to black freedom as they had ever been, and new laws made the lives of free blacks even more difficult. In 1792, South Carolina began requiring all free people between ages sixteen and sixty to register and pay a special tax. The courts had the power to levy a substantial fine on anyone who flouted the law and bind them out if they could not or would not pay—a penalty that could reduce a free black man or woman to a situation little better than slavery. Georgia did not lag far behind when it came to making free people register as free.

Holding on to liberty required constant vigilance and the stoic acceptance of demeaning and discriminatory laws regarding everything from dog ownership to nighttime curfews. It meant abiding by certain social conventions, for instance, always giving a white person the right of way in the street. Nevertheless, some free people fared better in South Carolina and Georgia, where whites had never seriously contemplated wholesale emancipation, than they did in the Upper South. They derived a measure of protection from their ties to prominent white families, even when no one openly acknowledged that those ties existed. The practice of emancipating concubines and biracial kin had begun in colonial days and it continued. The laws on the books were strict. By 1820 in both South Carolina and Georgia only the legislature could confer freedom upon a slave. In spite of the almost total ban on manumissions, some owners ignored the law and permitted a favored slave to live as if he or she were free. However, a compliant slaveholder's heirs might decide to end the arrangement or an angry white neighbor might inform the authorities and someone who had long thought of themselves as free could wind up on the auction block. In some instances, "free" people of color discovered that they were in fact slaves because their mothers had never been legally emancipated and they had inherited their unfree status.

At the time of the 1790 census the Lower South comprised just two states, Georgia and South Carolina. By 1820, it was much larger and its plantation economy was beginning to fuel the growth of much of the nation. The introduction of Eli Whitney's cotton gin in 1794, as well as the demand for raw cotton in the factories of Great Britain, and the eagerness of Northern shippers and merchants to share in the riches of the Cotton Kingdom combined to transform many aspects of commercial life. None of this growth would have been possible without Thomas Jefferson's purchase of the vast Louisiana Territory in 1803. The doubling in size of the United States at the stroke of a pen profoundly altered the lives of free people of African descent.

The French were willing to sell the Louisiana Territory because they could not crush the rebellion on Saint Domingue. Napoleon Bonaparte had pressured the Spanish into surrendering the Territory to France in 1800 in the confident expectation that his army could regain control of Saint Domingue and force the slaves back to work on the island's sugar and coffee plantations. The farms of the Territory would produce the food to feed the island colony's slaves and their masters. Everything fit seamlessly together in Napoleon's grand scheme, until the French suffered a humiliating reverse on Saint Domingue and he decided to jettison the Territory now that he had no use for it. In 1803, American and French negotiators struck a deal in Paris and overnight the United States gained millions of acres of real estate. What President Jefferson and his administration paid little heed to was the complex racial situation the nation was inheriting.

The southern part of the Louisiana Territory was home to a numerous and thriving "free colored" population that had grown even larger as a result of the uprising on Saint Domingue. Many *gens de couleur* had headed to the United States. Many more had gone to New Orleans. As French-speaking Catholics they thought they would be happier there than in the overwhelmingly Protestant, English-speaking United States.

The Spanish authorities were already becoming uneasy about the free community of color in and around New Orleans. Even before the arrival of the *gens de couleur* from the West Indies, the number of free people was increasing and so was their assertiveness. The French were worried when they regained control of Louisiana from Spain. They distrusted both the refugees from Saint Domingue and the native-born free people, with their militia companies, their growing affluence, and their insistence that they had rights almost equal to those of their white neighbors. When the region changed hands yet again, the Americans were no less wary. Louisiana's free people of color presented a challenge to the growing idea in the United States that all individuals of African descent should be subordinate to whites in every facet of their lives.

In 1804, the U.S. government split the enormous Louisiana Territory in two to make it easier to administer. What is today the state of Louisiana became the Orleans Territory, while everything north of that became the Missouri Territory. In the Orleans Territory racial tensions simmered. Many whites, both long-term residents and newcomers from the United States, despised free people as a class and complained loudly to the newly-appointed territorial governor, William Claiborne, about their arrogance. The free people themselves assured Claiborne of their loyalty, adding that they looked forward to enjoying the same rights as other Americans now that they, too, were American citizens. Claiborne did not regard them as citizens, although he was cautious about telling them that. The members of the new territorial legislature were much more forthright. When the legislature met for the first time, representatives weakened significantly the "colored" militia companies and slashed away at the privileges of free people of color in general. They also made it far more difficult for owners to emancipate any more slaves. If the lawmakers could not actually re-enslave free people, they could at least limit the number of slaves who gained their freedom.

In 1811, a massive slave revolt erupted not far from New Orleans. Governor Claiborne turned not only to whites but to the mixed-race militiamen for help to put down the uprising. The "colored" forces performed well, and Claiborne was appreciative. The legislature was less enthusiastic. Although lawmakers knew they needed the militia companies, given that a war with Britain was looming, they still wanted them firmly under white control. If the rank and file militiamen were dangerous, the officer corps was even more threatening. Whites feared that every "free colored" officer was another Toussaint L'Ouverture. They could not grasp the fact that many of these elite men were themselves slaveholders, and they had as much to fear from a successful slave rebellion as any white slave owner.

The War of 1812 witnessed a true test of the courage and the loyalty of the free colored militia. In the autumn of 1814 General Andrew Jackson hurried to Louisiana to fend off a massive British assault on the Gulf of Mexico. Jackson realized that he had to gain the trust of the free colored militiamen. He also feared that if he did not call upon them to join him they might become so resentful that they would side with the British. He was right to consider the feelings of these proud fighting men. The shabby treatment they had received thus far had left them feeling highly indignant. Jackson made an impassioned plea to them as brothers-in-arms and as fellow Americans and they responded by taking up their weapons and marching out to join him and his troops.

The Battle of New Orleans produced mixed results for the militiamen. Jackson praised them for their valor, but he was powerless to get them the equal pay he had promised them. On the other hand, their willingness to fight prompted some white residents to look more favorably upon them. It was not only the heroism of the black and mixed-race soldiers in defense of New Orleans that weighed with white citizens. The spectacular commercial growth of the city after 1815 meant that free people of color with skilled trades became increasingly valuable to the economy. To keep them down, especially when they showed no signs of fomenting rebellions, might have resulted in an exodus of useful and productive artisans. The new law code that Louisiana adopted allowed free people to move about the state at will and testify against whites in court—rights people of color did not have elsewhere in the Lower South. It also assumed that light-skinned people were free unless there was overwhelming evidence to the contrary. Everywhere else in the region, the burden of proof of free status rested upon the individual man or woman of color. When the Louisiana legislature finally did enact a series of restrictive laws, it exempted those people who had lived in Louisiana prior to statehood.

The growth of the United States continued. Mississippi joined the Union in 1817 and Alabama in 1819. Slavery was firmly rooted in both states, and with the demand for cotton continually increasing, slave owners were not prepared to give up valuable members of their labor force. Free people of color made up a miniscule segment of the population. By 1820, Mississippi and Alabama had a combined total of 1,029 free people—fewer than Richmond, Virginia, which had 1,235. The free black communities of the two new states also had to confront some of the most draconian laws in force anywhere in the South.

The situation that free blacks in the southern half of the Louisiana Territory had experienced after the transition from Spanish and French control was replicated in Florida when it became part of the United States in 1819. Free men and women of color in Spanish Florida feared they would lose the privileges they had had under Spanish law and be scarcely any better off than the slaves. They were somewhat more fortunate, given that white racial attitudes, harsh though they were, permitted some members of the free colored community a little more latitude. After the transition to American rule, Mobile, which had been in Spanish Florida, became part of Alabama, but free people there retained certain rights and privileges. The same was true in Pensacola, even when Florida lawmakers hacked away at the rights of free people in general across the state. To be free in either Mobile or Pensacola did not make free blacks citizens in the same way that whites were, but it did mean that life was somewhat better than it was for free people elsewhere in the Lower South.

If the South proved treacherous terrain for free people to navigate, the Midwest did not prove much more hospitable. In the early years of the new century the Old Northwest was transformed from one large territory into separate territories, which eventually became states. Although the Northwest Ordinance explicitly banned slaveholding in any state formed out of the territory between the Great Lakes and the Ohio and Mississippi Rivers, the absence of slaves did not translate into a warm welcome for free blacks anywhere in the region. In 1803, Ohio entered the Union as a "free" state. It did so with a body of laws in place that barred African Americans from voting, holding public office, or serving in the state militia. The following year the legislature informed free blacks that if they wanted to live in Ohio they must post a $500 bond for every member of their household, including infants and children. The situation in neighboring Indiana was no better, while in Illinois some white residents thought they should be able to keep the slaves they already owned, regardless of what the ordinance said. Even though Illinois became a "free" state, the racial climate was distinctly hostile and its laws with regard to black people were very repressive. As difficult as life was for free black people throughout the Midwest, some braved those difficulties. When all was said and done, they had often endured just as much discriminatory treatment back East.

The territorial growth of the United States since the 1790s onwards had affected the population of the entire nation in economic and political terms, but whether or not a particular state joined the Union as "free" or "slave" obviously had a tremendous impact on black Americans. As the extent of slave territory increased, so did the demand for slaves. In the summer of 1807, Congress prohibited the importation of any more slaves into the United States after January 1, 1808. The opponents of slavery, black and white, were overjoyed. They believed this was the first step toward total emancipation. On New Year's Day 1808 free people of color from Boston to Baltimore celebrated and held services of thanksgiving in their various churches. The January First observances continued for a number of years until the realization dawned that the end of the overseas trade had given way to a brisk domestic slave trade. Slavery was not in its death throes, and slaveholders in the Upper South had endorsed the federal ban on importations because it drove up prices for their own slaves when they shipped them off for sale in New Orleans and the other major slave markets. It also encouraged unscrupulous individuals to claim as fugitives black men and women who were legally free. Every move that strengthened slavery jeopardized the liberty of every member of the free community of color. Outside the ranks of the most zealous opponents of slavery, most whites either did not understand or simply did not care. However, the implications of the spread of slavery were about to stir up a nationwide debate.

In 1817, Missouri first applied for statehood. It was the most northerly part of the Missouri Territory to seek to join the Union, and it did so after a period of uncertainty about the question of black freedom. The federal government had initially put the entire Missouri Territory under the jurisdiction of the Council of the Indiana Territory. Slavery was illegal in the Indiana Territory, and French-speaking slaveholders in the Missouri Territory at first feared that they would have to emancipate their slaves, but their fears were unfounded. Although the Missouri Territory did not have as many free blacks as the Orleans Territory, and they had traditionally not had as many rights, whites did not want to see their numbers increase. They also enacted harsh new law codes which spelled out to the region's free people of color that they were there under sufferance. In 1820, when the question of statehood for Missouri eventually came before Congress, an acrimonious debate ensued. If Missouri joined the Union as a slave state it would upset the balance between "slave" and "free" states. Eventually the different factions hammered out an agreement. Missouri joined the Union as a slave state, while Maine separated from Massachusetts to become a free state, thus maintaining the balance. The so-called Missouri Compromise also stipulated that slavery could not exist in any state organized north of 36° 30' North (the southern boundary of Missouri), while any state created south of that line could choose freedom or slavery.

In the welter of rhetoric from white politicians no one gave much thought to the plight of free people of color in Missouri, but no sooner had Congress voted to admit the state than Missourians drafted a constitution that gave the legislature the power to exclude all free people of color from other states. Congressmen from several northern states protested that that provision violated the "equal protection" clause of the United States Constitution. Missouri had to agree never to deny entry to anyone who was a citizen of another state—but of course it was a moot point whether any state recognized black people as citizens. Missouri formally achieved statehood, and free people of color found that for all the talk about "equal protection" and "rights and immunities" they were not wanted in Missouri, any more than they were in any other state. They might insist that they had rights, in common with other Americans, but everywhere they looked their rights were being "compromised" out of existence.

Beyond Congressional compromises and restrictive law codes, beyond census figures and lines on the map that separated "free" and "slave" states, we are left with the fundamental question of what liberty actually meant for black men and women. Very obviously it meant different things depending on location and status. The outlook of an individual who was freeborn and lived in a major Northern city was very different indeed from that of the newly-emancipated slave or the person who had, as Frederick Douglass described it, "stolen" him- or herself and was passing as free and hoping to avoid recapture. Clearly, one individual's experience of freedom was not that of another individual. Even people of the same age and gender, living in the same setting, experienced liberty differently. If we cannot know everyone's life story, we can at least discover from the wealth of data available to us— everything from court cases and birth, death, and marriage records to very personal firsthand accounts—something of what it meant to be a free person of color in the United States in the generation after independence.

On achieving freedom, one of the first actions people of color often took was to change their names. For runaways that was a wise move, while those who were legally free wanted to shed fanciful slave names like Pompey and Dido, or diminutives like Bill and Sally in favor of William and Sarah. Men and women who had only ever had a first name acquired that hallmark of freedom, a last name, whether it be a craft name (Carpenter, Baker), a common "Anglo" name (Williams, Allen, Jones), or a name that reflected their new status, Freeman being especially popular. Few took their owner's last name unless that owner had been exceptionally generous or unless they thought it might help them to claim a link to an influential white family.

Whether or not a man or woman stayed in a given locality once they were free depended on a host of different considerations. Some individuals went in search of long-lost family members. Others remained where they were because that was where their friends and relatives lived. People moved to hunt for work or stayed and put down roots because they believed their prospects were brighter in a place they already knew. The wider world was a threatening and lonely place for some ex-slaves, while for others it represented the chance to test the limits of their liberty. Although most free people remained close to the land, towns exerted a strong appeal for those who were inclined to try their luck in a very different environment. Urban life had its downsides, but in the generation after independence it was in cities and towns that a vibrant free black community life began to emerge.

Freedom meant the chance for black Christians to worship as they chose. While many African Americans continued attending churches their masters had compelled them to go to, now that they were free they expected better treatment than having to sit in the "Negro pew" and receive communion after everyone else. Some people stayed in the churches they were familiar with. Others searched for a spiritual experience that they felt had more relevance to their lives. They might find that within a church that welcomed all believers regardless of race, or they might opt to join an African-American church. To some white observers that freedom of choice signaled a profound change. The richness of black organized religion, and all the other aspects of black life that sprang from the churches, was something they found most disturbing. To the African-American women and men who filled the pews on Sundays and gathered on other days throughout the week to study, discuss their situation, and support one another in various endeavors, the churches were vibrant community hubs that "spoke" to their freedom.

A large part of the black church's "creation story" occurred in Philadelphia, the effective capital of the nation until the federal government moved to Washington, D.C. in 1800. The city was also home to a rapidly growing free black community. Richard Allen and Absalom Jones, two of the men who had played a pivotal role in the formation of the Free African Society, were devout Methodists, and Allen, already a noted preacher, had come to Philadelphia at the invitation of the white elders at St. George's Methodist Episcopal Church to work with the scores of black people who were attending Sunday worship.

Although Allen and Jones began talking about establishing a separate black church in the mid-1780s, they did not initially find much support from either black or white Philadelphians. Within a few years, however, an ugly confrontation over segregated seating at St. George's, the growth in size and independence of Philadelphia's black community, and pledges of help from prominent whites led to a change. The fact that most of their white friends were Episcopalians posed a problem for Allen and Jones. At first both declared that they could not abandon Methodism because they believed in its egalitarian principles, even if some of the whites at St. George's had shown that they apparently did not, but Jones eventually reconsidered and agreed to seek ordination as an Episcopal priest. St. Thomas's African Episcopal Church opened for worship in 1794. That same year Richard Allen established Bethel (later Mother Bethel) as a black congregation within the Methodist denomination. By 1810, black Presbyterians and black Baptists in Philadelphia had organized their own congregations.

Black churches sprang up in other communities throughout the North. New York City, with its fast-growing free population, was home to a number of churches affiliated with various denominations. Congregationalists were especially strong in New England. New Haven's Temple Street Church and Hartford's Talcott Street Church were major centers of African-American religious life. Boston's black residents went in fairly large numbers to the city's Baptist churches, but they often encountered discrimination. Finally, in 1805, with help from some white sympathizers, they established the African Baptist Church. A year later they built their own meeting house, which still stands today.

Tensions over white control of black Protestant congregations arose in many different settings and led to the founding of two new African-American denominations. In 1816, black Methodists from Philadelphia, Baltimore, and other communities in the North and Upper South assembled in Baltimore to form the African Methodist Episcopal (AME) church. Richard Allen became the first bishop. Soon afterward, groups of black Methodists in and around New York City created the American Methodist Episcopal Zion (AMEZ) church.

The Catholic Church wrestled with many of the same problems as the Protestant churches. There were substantial numbers of black Catholics in places with strong French and Spanish traditions, notably New Orleans, St. Louis, and Mobile. The influx of *gens de couleur* from Saint Domingue also strengthened the black Catholic presence in Baltimore, Charleston, New York, and Philadelphia. Catholics did not organize separate black congregations, though, and no men who openly identified as black received ordination as priests. Black and white, free and slave, worshiped together, sometimes harmoniously and sometimes not.

Through the black churches, and sometimes independently of them, free black community life grew richer and more varied. More mutual benefit societies emerged along the lines of the Free African Society and the Newport African Union. In the period immediately after independence there were perhaps a dozen in major population centers in the North. By 1820 there were hundreds. All the societies worked in a similar way. A group of women or men who belonged to the same church or worked in the same occupation got together, chose a name for their society, crafted a set of by-laws, and began contributing regularly to a common fund. If a member became sick or was unable to find work, that member could draw on the fund. If a member or a member's spouse or child died, the fund would pay for a decent funeral.

Organizing in the South posed more problems than organizing in the North because whites were suspicious of free people gathering together for any purpose, however laudable. People overcame those difficulties, though, and soon there were societies in Baltimore, New Castle, Delaware, and Washington, D.C. Further south, Charleston's community of color split along lines of racial heritage. Light-skinned men formed the Brown Fellowship Society, while darker-skinned men set up their own society.

The societies did more than help members and their families through tough times. They became the arbiters of moral behavior. No one wanted to extend benefits to someone, for instance, who drank heavily and was more likely than an abstemious member to fall ill or lose a job. The societies disciplined members for transgressions of one kind or another, told them to mend their ways, and expelled them if they ignored the warnings. In this respect the mutual benefit societies reinforced the message the churches were spreading, namely that members must live lives that were irreproachable— for their own good and the good of the community.

Free black men in many cities and towns in the North and Upper South proudly identified themselves as "African" masons. Whites on both sides of the Atlantic had enthusiastically joined the "craft" of Freemasonry in the early eighteenth century, dedicating themselves to the quest for enlightenment and perfectibility across the lines of faith. The tenets of Freemasonry said nothing about it being exclusively white, and lodges in sailor towns like London, Liverpool, and Bristol often admitted African-American mariners as brother masons.

Back in America, however, white lodges routinely rejected black candidates. In the spring of 1775, just before the Revolutionary War began, a group of fifteen free black masons in Boston decided to approach a British military "traveling lodge" to see if the members of *that* lodge would recognize them as brother masons. Prince Hall and his friends convinced the lodge's officers of their devotion to the principles of Freemasonry and received from them the necessary authorization to form their own lodge. Hall, a former slave, became the lodge's "master." In the postwar period the black masons of Boston secured a warrant from the Grand Lodge in Britain and with it the power to charter other lodges.

Free people in other communities sought Prince Hall's help. A committee of black men in Philadelphia wrote Hall and explained that they and their friends had been assembling for some time and hoped to create a lodge, but the white lodges in Pennsylvania had rebuffed them, claiming that if *they* became masons, black men in Virginia would want the same privilege. Hall helped them establish their lodge and install their first officers in 1797, the same year that he chartered another black lodge in Providence, Rhode Island. Soon there were other lodges in New York City, Baltimore, Washington, D.C., and Alexandria, Virginia, although that was as far south as African or Prince Hall Masonry spread for many years, given the prevailing hostility in the Lower South to independent black societies of any kind.

A major goal of the masons was the pursuit of knowledge, and that fit with many other initiatives free black people were taking—through the lodges, the churches, and through a host of self-improvement associations. Reading and writing were increasing in importance among Americans in general in the post-Revolutionary era, and for free people of color basic literacy held a special significance. It was a hallmark of liberty and independence. It was also a tool they could use to try to improve their situation in life. To be sufficiently educated to read the Bible and to be able to pick up a newspaper or a handbill and make out the letters said something about one's connection to the wider world, while to be able to sign one's name was as symbolic of freedom as having a name of one's own choosing to sign. A priority for many of the newly-formed black community institutions was setting up schools for black children and organizing evening classes for adults. Whites in some localities in the North and the Upper South supported the efforts of black churches and charitable groups, donating money and books, and even volunteering to teach. However, if some white people encouraged the aspirations of their black neighbors out of a religious or humanitarian impulse, others were deathly afraid of the notion of black literacy and what it might lead to.

What it did in fact lead to was a flood of petitions and pamphlets as free people used the power of the written word to defend themselves and their communities from libel and slander and articulate their desires and goals. In doing so, they posed questions that white people did not always care to answer. In his 1791 letter to Thomas Jefferson, for example, the self-taught mathematician Benjamin Banneker asked how the author of the Declaration of Independence could speak of his love of liberty while "detaining by fraud and violence so numerous a part of my brethren, under groaning captivity and cruel oppression."[2] Two years later, Jefferson was one of thousands of white people who fled Philadelphia when yellow fever struck. Many more stayed behind because they had nowhere else to go or because they had already contracted the deadly disease. Richard Allen and Absalom Jones mobilized the Free African Society, and eventually many other black men and women, to try to relieve the suffering of their white neighbors, at grave risk to themselves. Despite assurances to the contrary, blacks were not immune to yellow fever, and hundreds sickened and died. Once the crisis was past, white publisher Mathew Carey downplayed the dangers black people had faced—he was convinced they were in fact immune—and he pilloried them as thieving opportunists who had exploited the epidemic for personal gain, stealing from those they had nursed and demanding excessively high wages for any services they rendered. Allen and Jones responded forcefully and eloquently in their *Narrative of the Proceedings of the Black People*. Elsewhere black people refused to accept attacks upon themselves without answering back. In Boston, Prince Hall spoke out about the mistreatment of members of his community. In Baltimore, Daniel Coker laid out the arguments against slavery in his *Dialogue Between a Virginian and an African Minister*. Philadelphia's James Forten used his own money to print his *Letters from a Man of Colour*, his personal protest against a series of discriminatory laws the Pennsylvania Senate was considering. In the 1790s and early 1800s black people came into their own as writers and orators. They also proved adept at using the political process. They submitted petitions for redress of grievances to the state and local authorities and occasionally to the U.S. Congress. Even when those bodies refused to receive their petitions, as Congress did in 1799 when dozens of men of color in Philadelphia denounced the kidnapping of free people under cover of the fugitive slave law and asked for action on the part of the federal government to begin the nationwide abolition of slavery, black people succeeded in making their voices heard.

One intriguing aspect of free black life in this period is the extent to which people incorporated aspects of an African past into their various initiatives. Absalom Jones and Richard Allen and their friends had called their society the Free African Society, and people in Newport had called theirs the Newport African Union. As the number of groups grew, they took names like the Daughters of Africa, the Angola Society, the Baltimore African Female Society, the Daughters of Abyssinia, the Sons of Ethiopia, and so on. People organized "African" schools and "African" churches, and they spoke and wrote of themselves as "Africans." Until the movement was renamed in Prince Hall's honor after his death, black freemasonry was "African" freemasonry. How much this spoke to a shared memory of Africa on the part of those who had been born there or had parents who had been born there, how much to a feeling of pride in the greatness of Africa, and how much to a sense of separation from Americans of European ancestry is a matter of debate among scholars. In the 1830s, heated differences arose over naming practices, with some Northern black leaders urging the abandoning of "African" because that term, and others like it, perpetuated the notion among whites that black people were not truly "American." For the women and men who experienced freedom in the 1790s and early 1800s, though, this posed no ideological or philosophical dilemma. "African" was what whites called them and it was what they called themselves. "African" was synonymous with "black," and they had no quarrel with that. But the issue of "African-ness" and what it implied about a sense of racial and national identity became an increasingly complex one during the 1810s. The question of whether black people should leave America once they were free had sparked the debate between Philadelphia's Free African Society and the Newport African Union in the 1780s. It resurfaced three decades later, generating a fascinating "paper trail" that helps us explore the question of how free people saw their future unfolding.

The pivotal figure was Paul Cuffe, a man whose own sense of identity was complicated by his ancestry. He was the son of a West African father and a Wampanoag mother. His father had arrived in Massachusetts as a slave, while his mother's people had been living in Massachusetts for centuries. Sometimes Cuffe described himself as an Indian, sometimes an African, and sometimes as a "mustee," the child of black and Native American parents. By the early 1800s, though, when Cuffe had become a merchant captain and the owner of a small but impressive fleet of ocean-going vessels, most of the people he interacted with regarded him as black.

Paul Cuffe was a convert to Quakerism, a faith that attracted relatively few people of color in this period, despite the Quakers' antislavery stance. In Cuffe's case that religious affiliation was crucial because it linked him to the transatlantic world of Quaker reform. Quaker abolitionists on both sides of the Atlantic wanted to see Britain's colony of Sierra Leone thrive and prove to the world that Africa had more to export than slaves. They reached out to Cuffe as a successful black businessman and a fierce opponent of slavery and they explained to him the vital role they thought the colony could play in advancing the antislavery cause.

In 1811, on his own initiative, but with the active encouragement of his fellow Quakers, Cuffe visited Sierra Leone and talked with the black loyalists who had settled there. Then he sailed to England and met the officials who would need to approve any plan he formulated to take black Americans to the colony to help develop the local economy. After that, he began contacting friends in the various free communities in the United States. At first he emphasized the profits that those with cash to invest in trade with Sierra Leone could reap. Then he talked about recruiting black craftsmen to set up all kinds of workshops in the colony and introduce some much-needed skills. Finally, he began mulling over the promoting of large-scale black emigration from the United States. American slaveholders were always saying they dared not free their slaves because they would slaughter them in their beds. Cuffe disputed that. The slaves did not want revenge, only freedom.

But if the sticking point was where the freedmen should live, perhaps creating separate settlements for them in West Africa would hasten the abolition of slavery. Cuffe talked with white Quakers and with his extensive network of well-connected, well-educated, and well-to-do free men of color. He generated a lot of interest, but once war broke out between the United States and Britain in 1812, he and his supporters were powerless to move forward.

As the war raged, Cuffe and his friends, both black and white, began speculating about setting up their own colony. The British would probably not want thousands of African Americans to settle in Sierra Leone. At most they might welcome a couple of hundred. There would have to be a separate, American-sponsored colony. And perhaps there should be another colony somewhere on America's western frontier for black people who wanted to stay in the United States but live apart from whites. No one was talking about an exodus of the entire black population at this point. Cuffe and the people with whom he was swapping ideas simply agreed that if some black people chose to form separate settlements either in America's "western wilds" or in Africa they had every right to do so. If they preferred to stay where they were, that was their right as well.

In the early weeks of 1815 the U.S. Senate ratified the peace treaty with Britain and the war ended. Cuffe refurbished his favorite ship, the aptly-named *Traveller*, and sailed to Sierra Leone, taking almost forty free black emigrants with him. Setting up an American colony was something that might happen in the future. This party of emigrants was going to the British colony. When Cuffe eventually returned to the United States he did so with mixed feelings. Although the British had not helped him as much as he had hoped, his settlers were thriving. He urged his friends to find more settlers and help him raise funds to finance their passage to Africa.

Cuffe and his associates were not the only people contemplating the merits of African emigration. Robert Finley, a white minister from New Jersey, had friends in high places, among them Speaker of the House of Representatives Henry Clay and Andrew Jackson, the hero of the Battle of New Orleans, and in Washington, D.C. in December of 1816 he convened a series of meetings at which he brought together his friends—and their friends—to discuss the future of black Americans. Significantly, he did not invite any black people to participate.

The result of the meetings in Washington was the creation of the American Colonization Society (ACS), which had as its goal promoting the emigration of free people of color from the United States to a colony somewhere in Africa. Their writings and speeches indicate that at least some of the men who founded the ACS truly hoped that they were taking the first step to ridding America of slavery. Others were more concerned about ridding America of free black people. As for where Finley himself stood, he had assured Cuffe of his sincere belief that a separate colony would serve the best interests of the entire black community, enslaved and free. Cuffe had not read Finley's *Thoughts on the Colonization of Free Blacks*, so he did not know that Finley was deeply perturbed about the black presence in the United States. Finley dismissed out of hand the idea of a settlement in the American West. Black people must go to Africa. They did not belong in America as slaves or as citizens.

Within a matter of days free blacks in major cities in the North and the Upper South began responding to what they were reading and hearing about the ACS. Community leaders in Georgetown, Virginia, were the first to react. They denounced African emigration, but they argued for a settlement in the Missouri Territory. Meanwhile, in Philadelphia disagreement surfaced between the rank and file and those accustomed to speak for them. Paul Cuffe's longtime confidante James Forten was deeply involved in the wrangling. Forten did not want to leave America. A Revolutionary War veteran, he saw *his* future as linked to that of the republic he had helped create. He was prospering as a sailmaker and real estate speculator. He did concede, however, that there were some free blacks who were not faring well in America, or who simply wanted to try their luck elsewhere. At least initially, Forten and some of those closest to him, including Absalom Jones and Richard Allen, shared Cuffe's opinion that the American Colonization Society was a humanitarian undertaking and the white men behind it were dedicated to black freedom. When Finley visited Philadelphia, Forten and other black leaders met with him and endorsed his plan, at least as he outlined it.

Many other black people in Philadelphia disagreed. They insisted that African colonization was an insidious plot hatched by whites who supported slavery while at the same time fearing and despising free blacks. Before long, more statements from the ACS leadership convinced James Forten and other prominent people of color not just in Philadelphia but in communities from Boston to Baltimore that the organization was *not* committed to ending slavery or to giving free people a choice about going to Africa. Then Paul Cuffe, the one man who might have been able to push the enterprise in the direction that free people of color would have found acceptable, fell ill and died. The dream of a large-scale voluntary exodus, coupled with the freeing of every slave in America, died with him.

The ACS forged ahead regardless. With the endorsement of powerful politicians in Washington, it mounted an expedition to West Africa to pick a site for a colony. What resulted was the founding of Liberia. The colony proved to be anything but a land of milk and honey for those who volunteered to go there, and disease and disputes threatened the whole venture. Although word soon filtered back to the United States about the dire situation in Liberia, the ACS kept up its recruiting efforts. A war of words broke out between the advocates of colonization, the vast majority of them white, and its opponents, almost all of them free blacks. James Forten was particularly vocal, especially when ACS officers tried to pressure him to lead the exodus now that Paul Cuffe was dead. Some people of color did agree to go to Liberia, although never in the numbers the ACS hoped. In many instances they were slaves whose masters freed them only on condition that they emigrate. Of the freeborn, most who left did so because they were pessimistic about their prospects in America. However, the overwhelming majority of free people steadfastly refused to abandon their homeland for an uncertain future in Africa.

The debate over emigration and colonization was just one aspect of the complex nature of black freedom in the generation after independence. Hundreds of thousands of people had struggled out of slavery, only to find that liberty seldom meant for them what it did for whites. However they saw themselves, most whites saw them differently. Freedom had given them hope for the future. It had also brought them disappointment and disillusionment. In the generation that followed, the struggle to make freedom truly meaningful continued. Black people endeavored in many different ways to claim what they considered their birthright as Americans. They sought prosperity and education, a peaceful existence, and the chance to live where they chose and as they chose. They also sought to liberate the growing number of black Americans who did not even share with them in "half-freedom." *They* were "free"—after a fashion—but as long as so many other black people were unfree, their own freedom was less than complete.

CHAPTER FOUR

~

"We Will Have Our Rights"

Redefining Black Freedom, 1820–1850

The men and women of the first generation after independence fought with courage and persistence to make black freedom a reality. They won some remarkable victories, even as they weathered crises in their personal lives and in the lives of their communities. Many were poor. Many had loved ones who were still enslaved, and they themselves were often at risk of losing their liberty. However, they spoke up and they organized. Their message to white Americans was that black people could make good use of their freedom.

Their sons and daughters built on what their parents had achieved. They struggled to maintain and expand their communities. They demanded equal access to education for themselves and their children. They let white Americans know that they expected nothing less than equality. They had much to contend with, though. In the thirty years from 1820 to 1850 there was a rise in racial violence and the passage of discriminatory laws in state after state. The American Colonization Society remained active and drew support from whites of all social classes. The nation extended its boundaries significantly in the course of these three decades, and with the acquisition of more territory came the question of what rights, if any, free blacks could enjoy as they tried to move into America's borderlands in search of the same opportunities that white pioneers were seeking.

In spite of all the laws designed to keep them subordinate to whites, and in spite of the hostility they encountered, some free blacks achieved the "American Dream" of economic self-sufficiency. By the 1820s, the Lower South was home to black plantation owners like William Ellison and Anna

Table 4.1 Free Black Population by State and Territory, 1790, 1820, and 1850

	1790	1820	1850
Alabama	——	571	2,265
Arkansas	——	59	608
California	——	——	962
Connecticut	2,801	7,844	7,693
Delaware	3,899	12,958	18,073
District of Columbia	——	4,048	10,059
Florida	——	——	932
Georgia	398	1,763	2,931
Illinois	——	457	5,436
Indiana	——	1,230	11,262
Iowa	——	——	333
Kentucky	114	2,759	10,011
Louisiana	——	10,476	17,462
Maine	538	929	1,356
Maryland	8,043	39,730	74,723
Massachusetts	5,463	6,740	9,064
Michigan	——	174	2,583
Minnesota (territory)	——	——	39
Mississippi	——	458	930
Missouri	——	347	2,618
New Hampshire	630	786	520
New Jersey	2,762	12,460	23,810
New Mexico (territory)	——	——	22
New York	4,654	29,279	49,069
North Carolina	4,975	14,612	27,463
Ohio	——	4,723	25,279
Oregon (territory)	——	——	207
Pennsylvania	6,537	30,202	53,626
Rhode Island	3,469	3,554	3,670
South Carolina	1,801	6,826	8,960
Tennessee	361	2,727	6,422
Texas	——	——	397
Utah (territory)	——	——	24
Vermont	255	903	718
Virginia	12,766	36,889	54,333
Wisconsin	——	——	635
Total	**59,466**	**233,504**	**434,495**

Source: Federal Population Schedules for the Years 1790, 1820, and 1850

Jai Kingsley. In a number of instances these planters were the heirs of rich white men, and some of them benefited from the labor of slaves. They were not the only black slave owners in the South. When they had the means to do so, free people purchased their friends and family members out of bondage with the obvious intention of freeing them. However, the likes of Ellison and Kingsley owned slaves for the same reason that whites did—because they wanted their labor.

Besides the wealthy "free colored" planters of the Lower South, there were thousands of black men and women in other parts of the country who had toiled, struggled, and parlayed their way into the land-owning classes by the 1820s. But for every independent and successful African-American farmer there were countless more for whom land ownership was an impossible dream, who had neither the capital nor the credit to buy land. Some became tenant farmers. Others squatted on vacant land, as many whites did, in the hope that the rightful owners would never find out. The majority of free black rural dwellers belonged to the ranks of landless laborers. The fortunate ones earned a living wage. The less fortunate labored for little more than food and shelter.

Opportunities were few and far between for free people who left the land and tried to make a living at something other than farming. In freedom, people searched for gainful employment wherever they could find it. They were not afraid of hard work. That was all most of them had known. However, few had exited slavery with much in the way of resources. If they had skilled trades they could not be sure that whites who had employed them when they had been someone's "property" would hire them once they were free.

Whites in different parts of the country had different ideas about what free black people should and should not be able to do for a living. In the cities of the North and Upper South, white working men complained vociferously about job competition, and whites of all classes conspired to prevent African Americans from becoming financially independent. In New York City in the 1820s, residents began a campaign against black chimney sweeps. They had not complained when the sweeps had been slaves, but once they were free their calls of "Sweep O, Sweep O" as they paraded through the streets allegedly disturbed the peace. White New Yorkers demanded that all sweeps get licenses, and they tried to make sure that no licenses went to black men. Carters and draymen also needed licenses, and whites wanted to ensure that *those* licenses went only to whites. This pattern of exclusion occurred in many other cities besides New York.

Learning a trade often enabled a slave to work his way out of bondage, but he might well not be able to pursue that trade as a free man. Frederick Douglass's master had leased him out to work in Baltimore's shipyards as a caulker. After he escaped in 1838, Douglass headed to the port of New Bedford, Massachusetts, only to discover that no shipbuilder would employ him. In New Bedford, so he learned, skilled labor was the preserve of white men. That was the case in most communities in the North and the Upper South.

Despite the uphill battles they faced, free black men did work in the skilled trades and some of the more enterprising discovered that the best way to make money was to diversify. A carpenter might make coffins and then graduate to funeral directing, especially in localities where white undertakers scorned to touch black bodies. Plasterers might branch out and offer a range of decorating services. Plumbers and glaziers undertook all sorts of home repairs. Shoe- and boot-makers tackled other kinds of leatherwork. Sailmakers like Philadelphia's James Forten made tents and fire hoses. The list went on and on. One of the ironies of free black life was that there was often greater scope for black artisans in the Lower South. The tradition of white men establishing their biracial children in business meant that places like Charleston, Savannah, and New Orleans had more than their share of "free colored" craftsmen, and those craftsmen thrived in trades that men of color elsewhere could not enter. The shortage of white competitors also helped. Immigrants did not move to the Lower South in large numbers. White "gentlemen" recoiled at the idea of working with their hands, but they wanted fashionably tailored clothes, well-maintained carriages, elegantly catered social events, and so forth, and they turned to free people of color to provide those services.

Black people looked for opportunities wherever they could find them. So much depended on prevailing white attitudes about what occupations were appropriate for free people. Possibly because it resembled domestic service, whites in every part of the country were happy to let African Americans cook and retail food. Black street vendors abounded. Women sold pepperpot soup, a spicy delicacy that urbanites purchased by the cup. They baked cakes and pastries, sweet and savory pies, tarts and cookies. In coastal cities black men operated oyster cellars, shucking and preparing oysters in many different ways and supplying their white customers with copious amounts of whiskey to wash the oysters down.

A number of African Americans distinguished themselves as caterers. In Philadelphia, Robert Bogle, John Appo, Henry Minton, and the Duterte clan were famous for their culinary skills. In Salem, Massachusetts, anyone wanting to host a fashionable dinner party engaged John Remond. In New York, the Esteve and Downing families provided fine food and impeccable service. Caterers moved into event planning. Robert Bogle, for instance, garnered praise from upper-class whites for tackling anything from a wedding to a funeral with equal finesse.

Astute individuals parlayed their expertise into various endeavors. Robert Roberts, the butler to a prominent white family in Massachusetts, published a book that guided household staff through everything from how to carve a duck to how to sober up an intoxicated gentleman. On the steamboats that plied the nation's great rivers, black stewards oversaw an extensive patronage network as they shopped for provisions to feed the passengers on their elegant "floating palaces." In Charleston, South Carolina, the Jones family ran a hotel that upper-class whites praised as the epitome of gracious living. African-American hoteliers operated fashionable hotels in other Southern cities, including the nation's capital. Of course, they could never think of renting a room to a person of color, however rich and respectable. If they did, they would lose all of their white guests.

Barbering was a mainstay of thousands of black men. Whites felt comfortable with black barbers. Somehow it seemed fitting that African Americans should be dutifully attending to the personal needs of whites. The occupation of "barber" covered everyone from the man with a few combs and razors to the likes of the Clamorgans of St. Louis, who oversaw an upscale establishment where they not only shaved their male customers but bathed them and sold them fine imported soaps and perfumes, razors and strops, mirrors, and hair tonics. Ladies could not enter the part of the premises where brothers Louis, Henry, and Cyprian Clamorgan superintended a small army of bath attendants and masseurs, but they could shop in the front section of the store, where Harriet and Julia Clamorgan helped them select hair ornaments, home furnishings, and toys for their children.

Black people opened stores in communities large and small, although few enjoyed the same degree of success as the Clamorgans. Neighborhood groceries attracted both black and white patrons, especially if they sold alcohol. African Americans also entered the secondhand clothing trade. Cast-off clothing functioned as a supplement to servants' wages. A lady's maid or a gentleman's valet expected to receive an employer's unwanted apparel, which they promptly sold to a dealer. A middle-class white patron browsing a used clothing store like the one David Walker ran in Boston in the 1820s could pick up last season's fashions at discounted prices.

Some enterprising black women operated "intelligence offices" or employment agencies, relying on their connections to elite white families to place people in domestic service. Others generated extra cash by taking in boarders. If a woman was already cooking and cleaning for her own family, having one or two extra household members did not greatly increase her already heavy workload. African-American women did laundry. Washing and ironing mounds of clothing was labor-intensive, but it was also work a woman could do at home while she watched over her children. The same was true of sewing. Seamstresses earned a pittance, though, and trying to sew a straight seam in poorly-lit rooms cost many their eyesight.

The talented needle-woman who advanced from seamstress to *modiste*, or designer, was in an entirely different class. As a slave in St. Louis in the

1840s, Elizabeth Keckley supported her master's entire family, so great was the demand for her gowns. Eventually Keckley amassed the extravagant sum her owners insisted on for her own and her son's freedom. Then she headed to Washington, D.C., where she knew that politicians' wives would pay handsomely to dress in the height of fashion. Some African-American women became noted milliners, copying the latest styles from Paris and London from illustrated newspapers. Others were in demand as hairdressers. They did "hair work," supplying affluent white women with false ringlets and curls in an era when a society lady expected her hair to be truly a work of art. The Remonds of Salem, Massachusetts—Nancy Lenox Remond and her daughters—were skilled coiffeurs, while New York native Eliza Potter trained in France and England and regularly spent the "season" working at Saratoga Springs and other exclusive resorts before settling in Cincinnati and opening her own salon.

White men often sought the status that came with being lawyers or physicians, but black people could seldom enter the learned professions. There were only two black lawyers in the antebellum era, Robert Morris and John S. Rock, both of them based in Boston. Prospective lawyers usually studied the law by apprenticing with a practicing attorney. However, few white attorneys were prepared to take on African Americans as law clerks, let alone make them partners once they passed the Bar.

As for formal medical education in this period, an aspiring doctor often learned from an established physician, serving an apprenticeship in much the same way as a young lawyer would. However, if he had the money and the inclination to do so, he might also enroll in one of the nation's growing number of medical schools. Those were the options for a white man planning to become a medical doctor. The choices were far more limited, though, for a black man who wanted a career in medicine. Medical schools routinely refused to admit African-American students and most white doctors did not want to risk alienating their white patients by taking on black trainees. James McCune Smith coped with those exclusionary policies in the 1830s by studying in Scotland, while John S. Rock found a sympathetic white doctor to train with (and achieved the distinction of qualifying as both a doctor and a lawyer). Even with the coveted M.D. in hand, a black physician still had to set up a practice. Only in a city with a large black middle class could he hope to succeed. For black women the challenges were even greater. Nevertheless, a courageous few refused to be deterred. One brave pioneer was Philadelphia's Sarah Mapps Douglass. Appalled that so many black women were ignorant of the basics of reproductive and pediatric health, Douglass talked her way into the Quaker-sponsored Female Medical College of Pennsylvania in 1853.

Then she purchased an anatomically correct "French mannequin" and began giving lectures to all-female audiences.

Although few black women and men became full-fledged M.D.s, many were respected healers. The annual trade directories of communities in the North and the Upper South listed dozens of black purveyors of "cures" of one kind or another, most derived from a mix of traditional African, Native-American, and European "folk" remedies, but as likely to work as the treatment licensed physicians offered, and certainly cheaper. People in need often consulted these "doctors" out of desperation without regard to race.

Black midwives sometimes attended white women as well as black women. Although they were not "licensed" in the strict sense of the word, they enjoyed a reputation in their neighborhood for their skill and compassion. While midwifery was the exclusive preserve of women, African Americans of both sexes provided other medical services. In an age when even the most highly regarded white physicians touted bleeding as a cure-all, some blacks trained to take blood by applying blood-sucking leeches or using "scarifying" blades to open a vein. The Pennsylvania Abolition Society's 1838 *Register of the Trades of the Colored People of Philadelphia* listed more than a dozen bleeders. One of them, Jacob C. White, kept detailed accounts of his practice in the 1830s and 1840s, and those accounts reveal that he treated men and women, black and white. His patients could not afford the services of an M.D., but they knew that "Doctor" White provided good care and his fees were reasonable.

In addition to bleeding people, Jacob C. White worked as a dentist. He was not the only African-American man to do so. At the most basic level, that of tooth-pulling, a dentist only needed a strong wrist. However, dentistry was evolving, with fillings, false teeth, and (most horrifying of all in an era before anesthesia or antisepsis) dental implants. Some black men became proficient, and the people who patronized them were likely to be as pleased with the results as those who went to white dentists.

The church drew hundreds of talented men of color, but whether a clergyman belonged to a predominantly white denomination or one of the emerging black denominations, he could seldom support himself and his family just by ministering to the spiritual concerns of his parishioners. A few, like future AME bishop Daniel Alexander Payne, ran private schools. Others doubled as shoemakers and carpenters, barbers and common laborers. A wife who was a wage earner was a real asset. Marriage was about more than setting a good example to one's flock. It required the income of a wife, and often a couple's older children, to enable a minister's household to survive financially.

Teaching attracted African Americans as it did whites, but finding job openings was far from easy for black men, and even more challenging for black women. Some people began their own fee-paying schools, and white antislavery organizations like the New York Manumission Society and the Pennsylvania Abolition Society made efforts to recruit black instructors for the schools they sponsored. The reality was, though, that there were many more qualified black teachers than there were positions available.

Other people of color tried to establish themselves in the arts, with varying degrees of success. Robert Douglass Jr. was an accomplished portrait painter who studied in London before returning home to Philadelphia and opening his own portrait studio. Most of the commissions he received were not for portraits, though, but for tavern signs and other ornamental work. To make a living Douglass took whatever came his way. There were African-American composers and musicians as well as painters. Philadelphia's Francis (Frank) Johnson composed music for elite white social events and he traveled extensively with his orchestra. He even went on tour to Europe in the mid-1830s—after an unsuccessful bid to get a passport. The State Department informed Johnson that it could not issue him one because he was black and hence not an American citizen. While the lack of a passport did not prevent Johnson from traveling overseas and reentering the United States, it denied him the services of the local American consul if he ran into trouble abroad. Johnson made his European tour anyway and, American citizen or not, in England he was invited to play for Queen Victoria. As for the theater, white audiences in America would not accept black actors, even in the lowest of comedy roles. In 1821, a couple of black impresarios in New York City made a small dent in that racial barrier when they opened the African Grove Theater. The fate of the theater is shrouded in mystery. It may have burned down, been closed by the authorities, or failed finan-cially. Whatever the case, no other black-owned theater replaced it. Its most gifted performer, Ira Aldridge, found fame as a Shakespearean actor, but he had to go to Europe to do so. Few men of color could contemplate a career like Aldridge's or Johnson's. They lacked the formal education to enter the professions, or the money to begin their own businesses. The difficulty of securing apprenticeships, combined with the prejudices of many of their white neighbors, put all but the most menial work beyond their reach.

However, in a setting in which job discrimination was the rule rather than the exception, one occupation was open to all. Seafaring was tough and dangerous, but captains usually hired crew members based on experience, not skin color. Racial segregation was impossible on even the largest merchant ship, and sailors knew their lives depended on getting along with one another. While shipboard life was not immune to the racial tensions that were so common ashore, in the seafaring fraternity the major division was between officers and men, not between blacks and whites. A few black men, like New Englanders Paul Cuffe and Absalom Boston, even became ship owners and merchant captains. What no man of color could do, however, was to enlist in the U.S. Navy. Although black sailors had served with distinction in the Revolutionary War and the War of 1812, by the 1820s the official Navy policy was that blacks could only be cooks or stewards.

Back on land, African-American men took whatever work they could find. What they often got, if they were employed at all, was work that was unpleasant, strenuous, and poorly paid. An especially unpalatable form of employment in the days before flush toilets was removing the contents of privies. Because they carted sewage through the streets at night, people referred to them euphemistically as "night soil men." The complaints of white householders in New York and elsewhere centered on two aspects of the "trade"—the tendency of "night soil men" to wheel their stinking carts past their homes (the carts had to go *somewhere*) and their habit of calling out as they went along to advertise their services.

Black men also did much of the heavy lifting in urban communities. They worked as porters and stevedores. They cleaned streets and dug graves and privies. They groomed horses and blacked boots. They toiled at anything and everything, and some turned to crime when they could find no other way to make money. For every free man who established a business or entered a skilled trade, a hundred more were common laborers. If they were fortunate, they were hired by the week or the month. Many, though, were day laborers. They would turn up before dawn to wherever they heard someone was hiring workers, though all too often employers passed them over in favor of whites. They could only hope that they would be luckier the next day.

In common with black men, most free black women found themselves relegated to low-paying and onerous "day work." In their case that meant domestic work, and that entailed juggling family responsibilities with the demands of one's employers. An added burden came from prevailing notions of female propriety. "Ladies" seldom ventured outside their homes, unless in the company of male relatives. "Women" were in a different category. A woman hurrying through the streets on her way to and from work frequently received insults from white men who assumed that any unaccompanied woman, especially a black woman, was a prostitute.

In truth, selling sex was something that some women, regardless of race, resorted to. Every town had its red light district, where women and girls bartered sex for money in dingy alleyways and in upscale bordellos. A few grew rich as madams. Generally, though, violence, disease, and harassment by the officers of the law were the lot of those who plied the sex trade.

At the other end of the spectrum was the woman of color who lived with a white man in a long-term relationship. In and around New Orleans, *plaçage* was a recognized social institution. A white man would select a young mixed-race *placeé* or "companion" at one of the city's famed "quadroon balls" and offer to provide for her and any children their relationship produced. The arrangement might endure lifelong or terminate when he married or tired of her.

New Orleans was notorious for the extent of "race mixing" that went on there, but it was common in other Southern communities as well. Free women of color might be coerced into sexual relationships that had little to do with mutual attraction and everything to do with money and power. Others chose freely to live with well-to-do white men. The mother of the enterprising Clamorgans of St. Louis parlayed her youth, her beauty, and her wit into cash. Although Apoline Clamorgan was legally free, her white father had left her very little to live on. As she saw it, she had two options—she could accept an offer of marriage from a free man of color and most likely end up as a household drudge for a white family, or she could take a white lover. Apoline chose cohabitation and comfort over marriage and poverty. She entered into a series of liaisons and her children inherited from her the money to start their own business.

There were notable success stories among free people of color in the antebellum era, but how well African-American women and men in any particular community fared depended on a host of factors, most of which were beyond their control. When the economy was robust, they shared (although not equally) with whites in the general prosperity. When it took a downturn, they suffered disproportionately. Since they were invariably the last hired, they were the first fired. A family's income obviously determined where and how well that family lived. Residential segregation existed in most urban areas in the antebellum era, but what separated people was less often race than money. "Middling" and affluent people of color lived alongside whites of the same social and economic status, and their interactions might be friendly or hostile, depending on circumstances. The urban poor, regardless of race, rented badly maintained homes in narrow alleys and courts where the sun rarely shone. Overcrowding and inadequate sanitation led to disease. It took time for local boards of health to accept that epidemics spread not because of race or ethnicity—they blamed Irish immigrants as well as free blacks—but because of deplorable living conditions. Malnourished, inadequately clothed, and lacking access to basic health care, the poor were more prone to illness, and when they contracted cholera, influenza, yellow fever, or any of a host of other ailments, they infected their less impoverished neighbors.

Joseph Willson had grown up in a wealthy mixed-race home in Augusta, Georgia. In the mid-1830s he moved to the North, trained as a printer, and distinguished himself as a writer. One of his goals was to enlighten white people about their black neighbors. It irked him that whites were "accustomed to regard the people of color as one consolidated mass." As he explained, some free people lived "in ease, comfort and the enjoyment of all the social blessings," some "in the lowest depths of human degradation," and a great many "in the intermediate stages." The free black population Willson described was complex and multilayered. Most of its members had hope for the future, and they expressed that hope not only within their own families but in the rich communal life they worked so hard to foster. If they were people "in between" in so many senses, they devoted a tremendous amount of energy to making that marginal space between slavery and full freedom as intellectually and spiritually satisfying as they could. Willson knew, though, that they could not afford to be complacent. Too many white people in both the North and the South did indeed see them as "one consolidated mass" and insisted that the nation would be better off without them.[1]

One of the fiercest battles free black people had to fight in the 1820s and beyond was over their right to remain in the United States. Their fears about the American Colonization Society proved well-founded. The conviction grew among whites that free blacks did not truly belong in the United States, and they began urging their state legislatures to appropriate funds to promote African colonization. They also called on lawmakers to restrict the rights of free blacks in order to reinforce to them the message that they had no future in America.

African Americans in the Upper South were as zealous in trying to thwart the Liberia scheme as those in the North were. In Baltimore, for example, people of color routinely followed white ACS agents around town, anxious to make sure that they did not find any recruits, and even coaxing would-be emigrants off ships in the harbor. The ACS did enlist some enterprising individuals, like John Jenkins Roberts, a Virginia-born merchant whose education and business contacts enabled him to do well in Liberia and eventually become its first president. However, while some free blacks did agree to go to Liberia, most wanted nothing to do with the ACS.

Not everyone who rejected the Liberia scheme opposed voluntary emigration. In the mid-1820s, Haitian president Jean-Pierre Boyer made lavish promises to induce American free blacks to settle in his country. Throughout the North, the Upper South, and the Midwest, free people enthusiastically endorsed the idea of moving to a nation that had come into being as the result of a successful slave uprising. Perhaps as many as ten thousand left for Haiti between 1824 and 1826. They left with high hopes, only to be bitterly disappointed when they discovered that they were pawns in a high stakes game of international diplomacy. Boyer reasoned that if he took in an unwanted segment of the American population he could persuade the United States government to recognize Haitian independence. Although some of the African-American emigrants stayed in Haiti and prospered, most found that they were as poor there as they had been in the United States and they soon returned home.

Despite the failure of the Haitian scheme, individually and collectively black people continued to leave the United States in search of brighter prospects elsewhere. An unknown number went to Canada. Some were runaways who knew that the Canadian authorities usually refused to hand over people whose only offense was seeking freedom. There were also groups of refugees who concluded that even though they were legally free they could not remain in the United States. In 1829, in response to growing violence from the city's white street gangs, hundreds of free people in Cincinnati moved to Canada where they organized their own farming community with the encouragement of the Governor-General. Although they endured many hardships, their initial settlement grew and more settlements followed, attracting black émigrés not only from Ohio but from all over the United States. Other people of color who crossed over into Canada headed for urban areas like Toronto.

After Britain abolished slavery throughout its empire in 1833, some African Americans set sail for Jamaica, or Trinidad, or British Guiana (today's Guyana). In all three colonies planters were crying out for labor and assuring settlers that in a year or two they could become independent landholders. As was the case with the Haitian scheme, most of the emigrants were disappointed, but a few did well. Back in the United States, black leaders hesitated to condemn resettlement programs in principle, insisting that free people had the right to go wherever they wished. What they denounced was the growing racism that was making emigration not so much a choice as a necessity.

Racial tensions had never been far below the surface, but during the 1820s and 1830s harassment and sporadic acts of violence exploded into full-blown race riots in the North and the Midwest. There was no shortage of white-on-black violence in the South. In the aftermath of Nat Turner's slave rebellion in Virginia in 1831, whites vented their fury on free blacks, who, they insisted, must have conspired with the rebels. In Raleigh,

North Carolina the authorities put every free black man in jail, a violation of their rights that probably saved their lives. Across the Upper South, scores of innocent free blacks suffered at the hands of white vigilantes, though what happened outside the South in the 1820s and 1830s was even worse. A verbal altercation or an unsubstantiated rumor about "unacceptable" behavior on the part of a black person or a group of people was usually all it took to inflame the mob. In 1824, rioters destroyed black homes in Providence, Rhode Island on the pretext that there was prostitution going on in the area. In 1826, white rowdies attacked black dwellings on the northern slope of Boston's Beacon Hill. The 1829 Cincinnati riot was at least in part a response to job competition and the sense that black people were prospering at the expense of whites. Although many other places experienced episodes of violence, the epicenter was Philadelphia, which endured four bloody and destructive riots in fifteen years.

A major source of contention was access to public spaces. Black Southerners understood that only too well. Whites were far less likely to molest a slave going about his master's business with the appropriate pass than they were a group of free blacks gathering for any purpose, however innocent. In cities like Baltimore and Washington, D.C., free people seldom assembled in large groups, even if they had the permission of the authorities to hold a parade or march in the funeral procession of a respected community leader. People in the Lower South exercised even more caution. African Americans outside the South were bolder. They persisted in claiming the same rights as whites. They had occasions, some of them solemn and others festive, that they wanted to mark by taking to the streets, but the sight of such public displays of community strength often provoked an angry reaction from whites.

The violence of the urban mob was one aspect of white hostility free people had to confront. The passage of discriminatory laws was another. The legal restrictions African Americans faced in their everyday lives were both expensive and demeaning. In 1821, the District of Columbia required that all free blacks register annually and post a bond to ensure their "good behavior." Free people in North Carolina were supposed to wear a shoulder patch with the word "Free" on it. Throughout the Upper South, free blacks were forbidden to trade in certain commodities, their interactions with slaves were closely regulated, and the list of occupations off-limits to them grew steadily. Not everyone complied. People neglected to register. They pursued trades officially closed to them, traveled where they were not supposed to, and associated with enslaved friends and family members. However, they always had to worry that the authorities would crack down.

Further south the situation was worse. In 1822, whites in South Carolina panicked when they learned what free black carpenter Denmark Vesey had planned—nothing less than the freeing of all the slaves in and around Charleston, and (so it was rumored) the slaughter of every one of Charleston's white inhabitants. Vesey seemed an unlikely rebel. It never occurred to white Charlestonians that Vesey was free only because he had bought himself with his winnings from a lottery. Almost all of his family members remained enslaved. The authorities executed Vesey and the slaves he had plotted with, but they worried that the free community of color contained many more Veseys just waiting for an opportunity to subvert the slave system. Henceforth, they decreed, no free person of color who left South Carolina could ever return. As an additional safeguard, every free black male over the age of fifteen had to have a white guardian.

Throughout the South, free people resorted to all sorts of subterfuges to protect themselves and their families from discriminatory laws. James Thomas recalled how his mother had navigated around the Tennessee law that said that all newly emancipated slaves must leave the state. Sally Thomas ran a laundry in Nashville and she managed to save enough money to buy her son, although she herself was still a slave. She did not want the authorities to take James away from her once they learned he was free, so she enlisted the aid of a sympathetic white neighbor who assumed ownership of the boy in a fictitious "sale." Years later, when James Thomas was a successful businessman, the neighbor "freed" him and endorsed his petition to the courts to be allowed to remain in Tennessee.

Even if a state did not act to control the free black community, a locality within that state might do so. For example, in St. Louis any free black person not born in Missouri needed a license to live in the city, and that could cost as much as one thousand dollars. The St. Louis court records reveal the intricate webs of friendship that developed as people assisted one another to get their licenses. In the early 1830s, Harriet Thompson, a Pennsylvania native, wed barber Henry Clamorgan. He was exempt from the residency law because he was a Missouri native, but Harriet was not, and the couple recruited several people to post cash bonds with the court on her behalf. Likewise, Henry helped Harriet's sister Mary to obtain a license later when she married his best friend, Samuel Mordecai.

Robert Jerome Wilkinson, another member of the Clamorgans' circle, learned what happened to those who refused to obey the law. Citing the "equal protection" clause of the U.S. Constitution, Wilkinson argued that if whites did not need a license, he should not need one. He was promptly arrested. After several weeks of incarceration he abandoned the fight, paid for his license, and settled down in St. Louis. He was lucky. The authorities could have expelled him, or even bound him out to pay his fine. In many parts of the South the courts routinely bound out black lawbreakers, some of whom ended up in slavery when unscrupulous employers sold them.

Wholesale kidnapping without the cover of the law was also a constant danger. Just as the Underground Railroad spirited slaves to freedom, so another, less well-known "railroad" conveyed free people into bondage in the South. Every year organized gangs and "freelancers" seized unsuspecting individuals and hustled them away. Sometimes black Northerners went to the South looking for work and were ensnared. That was the plight of New Yorker Solomon Northup, who endured twelve years of enslavement in Louisiana. It was the fate of scores of Northern black sailors whose vessels called at ports in the Lower South. The local laws stipulated that African-American sailors had to stay in jail while their vessels were in port. Once they were in jail, a dishonest captain or jailer might be tempted to sell them as slaves. Kidnappers would even seize white people and claim they were "bright mulattoes." If an individual was reputed to be black, that made his or her evidence inadmissible against whites in most Southern courts.

The erosion of black people's fundamental rights continued inexorably, but so, too, did the efforts of African Americans to challenge the discrimination they faced. They attacked segregation, especially on public transportation, which was a class issue as well as a racial one. Poor blacks did not travel much. If they had to go across town they walked, and if they needed to go further afield they could only afford the cheapest accommodations—precisely the ones white-owned shipping lines and railroad and streetcar companies earmarked for them anyway. Affluent people felt the sting of unequal treatment more intensely, so they campaigned against it. They refused to give up first-class seats and steamboat berths they had paid for. They pointed out that black servants could travel with white employers, but black fare-paying passengers were forced into the "colored car" or refused passage.

What stirred up even deeper resentment than segregation was the denial of rights by the state and federal governments. If black Southerners were more reluctant to speak up for fear of retribution than were Northerners, they were no less eager to secure their rights. The right on which free people focused most intently was the right to vote. This right, they contended, was the key to all others, and yet almost every new state that entered the Union after 1820 barred them from voting, while many of the older states disfranchised them. By 1850, only 6 percent of the nation's free black men lived in states where they could vote on the same basis as whites.

When African Americans had leverage they used it. In an era before the secret ballot, those who employed whites, rented homes to them, or patronized their businesses could "advise" them about whom to vote for and hint at repercussions if they did not heed that advice. Of course, few black people could wield that kind of power, and indirect influence was no real substitute for the right to vote. Understandably, African Americans grew angry as they watched white immigrants become naturalized and qualify to vote while they could not.

The nation's free people of color mulled over how to respond most effectively to the racial oppression they were experiencing—oppression that seemed to grow in intensity with each passing year. Black leaders from across the Northern and Midwestern states began holding meetings to review the situation of the entire black community, free and enslaved, and try to devise strategies for improving it.

What prompted the calling of the first black national convention in 1830 was the plight of Cincinnati's African-American community in the wake of the previous year's rioting. The consequent flight of hundreds of black people to Canada constituted a humanitarian crisis that people of color elsewhere could not ignore. Organizers dispatched invitations to different communities, and several dozen men gathered at Philadelphia's Mother Bethel Church. They pledged to do whatever they could for the Cincinnati refugees and then they turned to what black people across the nation needed, namely an end to slavery and racial inequality. There was so much to discuss that they agreed to meet again the following year. The pattern of annual meetings continued through the early 1830s until the delegates began fighting among themselves over goals and tactics and the national convention movement weakened and died. In the 1840s, though, community leaders decided that they must sink their differences and revive the movement. White hostility was growing and they needed to present a united front. Disagreements and personality clashes occasionally disrupted the proceedings, but through the 1840s and beyond the black national conventions were scenes of dynamic and energetic debate. Black people in individual states also organized their own conventions to discuss regional and local matters.

Beyond the national and state conventions, other meetings took place. The African Methodist Episcopal (AME) and the AME Zion denominations held regular assemblies of ministers and prominent laymen, and matters of church policy spilled over into discussions about civil rights. Beginning in the early 1830s, black men met with white men in the annual conventions of national and state antislavery organizations. For years women were excluded, so they held their own conventions. Just as the AME and AMEZ meetings were not limited to matters of religion, so the women's antislavery conventions were not limited to abolition. Black and white women started to focus on their status as women and link the ending of racial oppression to the ending of gender discrimination.

The black men and women of the post-Independence era had seized on the power of the written word, and their sons and daughters built on the foundation they had laid. They wrote antislavery verse and personal memoirs, attacks on unjust laws, and treatises on everything from Christian theology to the role of African Americans in the Revolutionary War. By far the most inflammatory publication by a black writer, at least as far as the defenders of slavery were concerned, however, was David Walker's *Appeal to the Coloured Citizens*. When it appeared in 1829 it provoked outrage among slave hold-ers while inspiring people of color by its boldness. Walker was from North Carolina, the son of a free woman and a slave. His *Appeal*, written long after he had relocated to Boston, demonstrated his voracious appetite for reading and his ability to construct devastatingly effective arguments. Why, he thun-dered, should black people endure the slave owner's lash one moment longer? And why should any free person be satisfied with the "very *dregs*" of liberty, when they deserved nothing less than full citizenship?[2] When copies of his *Appeal* surfaced in the South, lawmakers demanded that the authorities in Boston silence Walker. Boston's mayor responded that Walker had not broken any Massachusetts law. In little over a year, however, Walker *was* silenced. Although rumors circulated that he had been poisoned, recent scholarship has uncovered the true cause of his death, tuberculosis. Perhaps Walker spoke out because he knew he did not have long to live under any circumstances. If his enemies did not kill him, the disease he was suffering from surely would.

In his short but eventful life David Walker promoted the twin causes of antislavery and racial equality in various ways. He is best known today for authoring the *Appeal*, but he was also the Boston agent for the nation's first black-owned and edited newspaper. The first issue of *Freedom's Journal* rolled off of the presses in New York City on March 16, 1827. *Freedom's Journal* printed a wide range of items, from denunciations of slavery and racial injustice to historical accounts of Africa, letters and opinion pieces, marriage and death notices, poetry, and advertisements. Many more people read *Freedom's Journal* than actually subscribed to it. Well-thumbed copies were handed around in churches and self-improvement societies, and among friends and workmates, few of whom paid a cent to keep the newspaper in business. Lack of revenue was one reason for its demise. Another was its editor's change of heart. In 1829, John Brown Russwurm shocked readers by announcing that he planned to emigrate. The college-educated Russwurm had accepted the American Colonization Society's invitation to edit a newspaper in Liberia. Shortly before his departure, he wrote confidently to a friend that "the day . . . is not far distant, when all our people . . . will be as anxious to locate themselves there [Liberia], as foreigners now are of emigrating to America."[3] He could not have been more mistaken, but in the short term his defection doomed *Freedom's Journal*.

White abolitionist William Lloyd Garrison's *Liberator* filled the void for several years. Garrison's black friends helped fund the newspaper, and Garrison published many articles by and about free people, as well as launching blistering attacks on the slave system in the South. Still, the *Liberator* was no substitute for a newspaper owned and edited by African Americans. Answering that need, in the 1830s and 1840s, African Americans launched numerous newspapers and magazines, including the *Colored American*, Frederick Douglass's *North Star*, and Philadelphia's *National Reformer*. By 1850, an African-American reader in the North or the Midwest with cash to spare, or a membership in one of the black literary societies, could read at least a couple of black newspapers and find out what was going on beyond the confines of his or her own community. But subscribing to a paper like the *North Star* in New York City or Chicago was one thing. Subscribing in Charleston or Savannah was quite another. Postmasters routinely pulled "incendiary" publications out of the mailbags and told the local authorities who the intended recipients were.

The sentiment grew among whites in the South that black literacy was dangerous. They feared that if free blacks became educated they would disseminate abolitionist literature, forge passes for their enslaved friends, and teach them to read and write. Although a number of states in the slave South passed laws expressly forbidding the education of free people, African Americans found ways around those laws. In Missouri, for instance, preacher John Berry Meacham reportedly held classes on a boat on the Mississippi, where he and his students were under federal rather than state jurisdiction. Charleston, South Carolina had a number of black schools, some of which flourished in secret, while others operated more openly. At least in the case of the Brown Fellowship Society, which sponsored the education of its members' children, the fact that many of those members had ties of blood to prominent white families, and some were slave owners themselves, earned the organization's endeavors grudging acceptance from the authorities. Elsewhere in major urban centers like Baltimore, New Orleans, and Washington, D.C., African-American schools did function, even if they had to do so without public funding and their trustees had to be constantly on their guard against suspicions that they were in any way threatening slavery.

In the North as well as the South, black education became more closely linked to the campaign for abolition and black rights in the minds of many whites, and that could have a chilling effect, as the fate of several educational initiatives made abundantly clear. In 1831, an interracial group of reformers chose New Haven, Connecticut as the site of the nation's first African-American college. The horrified townspeople organized a protest meeting and handed the plan a crushing defeat. In 1833, in Canterbury, Connecticut, white teacher Prudence Crandall agreed to admit the daughter of a prosperous African-American farmer to her private school. Almost immediately, white parents withdrew their daughters. Crandall responded by announcing that henceforth she would operate her school exclusively for "young ladies and little misses of color." Word spread, and affluent black parents in a number of Northern cities enrolled their daughters in Crandall's school.[4] The white inhabitants of Canterbury promptly embarked on a campaign of harassment that culminated in Crandall's arrest. Two years later, Noyes Academy, in Canaan, New Hampshire opened its doors to black as well as white students. The experiment ended abruptly when local whites chased out the black students and tore down the school building.

Black parents in the North and Midwest petitioned repeatedly for access to public education for their children. They pointed out that their tax dollars helped to pay for the schooling of white children. If the local boards of education listened, what they typically provided for black children were segregated schools housed in rundown buildings. Almost all of the teachers the boards of education hired to teach in black schools were white. Some were truly dedicated to improving the lives of their students, while others regarded assignment to a black school as a demotion and took out their frustrations on their pupils. As for the curriculum, it was usually much more limited than in white schools because the authorities assumed that black children were incapable of mastering anything beyond the fundamentals and they had no need of advanced education anyway because it would render them unfit for the menial occupations they would fill.

Some communities did integrate their schools, and black parents moved or sent their children to live with friends in those communities. Cleveland admitted students to its public schools without regard to race, and that attracted some out-of-state families. Thanks to pressure from black parents, school integration came to one town after another in Massachusetts, but the battle in Boston was a protracted one. In 1849, printer Benjamin Roberts sued the Boston School Board on behalf of his young daughter. Sarah Roberts's attorneys pointed out that Sarah had to pass a number of "whites only" schools each day on her way to the "colored" school. The Roberts case went down to defeat, although in 1855 political maneuvering led to the desegregation of public schools throughout the state, including Boston.

Black parents wanted good schools for their children and they themselves valued learning. Evening and Sunday classes for adults attracted many who had never had the chance of an education in their earlier years. Social and intellectual life in the African-American community flourished, even if it did so beyond the notice of most whites. Where they had the numbers and the means to do so, free people organized literary and debating groups. They had to do so separately from whites because even though many libraries and lyceums boasted that they were "free to all," in reality "all" did not include blacks. In an added irony, black men's societies excluded women, so African-American women formed their own literary groups. Members met regularly to read, to write, and to give one another encouragement. One activity blended into another. The women sewed or knitted garments for the "charity box" while one of their members read aloud to them. They discussed how best to help their community. They collected money to aid runaway slaves and they sponsored abolitionist fundraisers. For both the men and the women who flocked to literary societies, antislavery and campaigning for civil rights went hand-in-hand with the desire for education.

It is impossible to overemphasize the bitter reality of slavery in the lives of the overwhelming majority of free black people. Many had been slaves or had kinfolk who were enslaved. Even the freeborn understood that the existence of slavery made them vulnerable to kidnapping. Destroying slavery and securing full citizenship were the twin goals of free black activists. For some, the means to achieving those goals lay in organizing all sorts of initiatives, from antislavery societies to national and state-wide civil rights movements, from seizing the power of the press to petitioning, agitating, and endeavoring to shame the state and federal governments into acting justly to everyone, regardless of race. For others the tactic of choice was direct action when slave catchers or city constables seized an alleged runaway or a white mob seemed intent on driving black people out of their homes. In organizing or in using force, free people collaborated with white sympathizers when they could and acted on their own when they had to.

African Americans were almost always prepared to work with white abolitionists. The older organizations like the Pennsylvania Abolition Society and the New York Manumission Society did not admit blacks to membership. However, that "first wave" of white abolitionists did their best to improve the situation of people of color by sponsoring schools, helping people find work, and trying to rescue victims of kidnapping. Admittedly, they dispensed a good deal of patronizing advice, but most black people who interacted with them accepted that the white men in these organizations were well-intentioned.

Black activists in the North welcomed the rise of "radical" abolitionism among whites in the 1830s. They admired the fervor of William Lloyd Garrison and the members of his circle. They applauded the calls for immediate emancipation. They accepted invitations to join the American Anti-Slavery Society, and a number held office in the organization and in its state and local affiliates. After a few years, though, some black abolitionists became disenchanted when they realized that they were not necessarily equal participants.

The ties between blacks and whites in organized antislavery were complex. The older "whites only" societies often had a greater appreciation of the need to look beyond emancipation to the new social and economic patterns that would have to develop if black people were to be free in more than name only. Many white foes of slavery who joined the new antislavery societies found it easier to focus on ending Southern bondage than on working toward racial equality. Sarah Forten, the daughter of wealthy sailmaker James Forten, wrote of encountering "professed friends" within the ranks of the white abolitionists to whom prejudice "clings like a dark mantle." One man even confessed to her that he could remember the time "when in walking with a Colored brother, the darker the night, the better Abolitionist was I."[5] Although sometimes disappointed in their white allies, Forten and countless other people of color refused to abandon the abolitionist cause. Destroying slavery lay at the heart of their struggle to force the nation to live up to its founding principles of freedom and equality for all. They would simply have to convince white reformers that eradicating slavery was not good enough. If black people were stranded on the margins of American society, somewhere between abject slavery and full citizenship, then abolition would be a failure, or at best a partial victory.

While many members of the emerging free black middle class in the North and Midwest joined antislavery societies, people of color at all levels of society did whatever they could to weaken and ultimately destroy the institution of slavery. They contributed money to the Vigilance Committees that coordinated aid to fugitive slaves. Sometimes they helped not with cash but with a hint to an anxious-looking black stranger about a place to hide, the chance of a job or a hot meal. People in slaveholding states reached out when they could. If they recognized the wisdom of not openly affiliating with an antislavery society, they still found innumerable ways to assist fugitives.

Whether they lived in the South, the North or the Midwest, free people of color followed as intently as their white neighbors did the events that were unfolding on the nation's borders in the three decades after 1820. It was hardly surprising if those events held a special significance for them, because what was at issue was the fundamental question of black freedom.

That question arose in 1821, when Mexico declared its independence from Spain. Eager to attract settlers to the underpopulated state of Coahuila (which included Texas), the Mexican government invited in people from the United States. Many of those who took advantage of the offer of cheap land were white slaveholders. Although Mexico renounced slavery in 1829, the national government was willing to compromise on abolition and other issues with the American settlers in Texas. Compromise was not good enough for the Texans. Tensions escalated until 1835, when Mexico's head of state announced that he would tolerate no more defiance from the Texans and they responded by rejecting Mexican authority over them.

In the war that followed, the Texans emerged victorious. Texas became the Lone Star Republic, and it did so with the aid of free black men, like William Goyens, who was Texas leader Sam Houston's interpreter with the Indian peoples of East Texas, and dozens of others who fought for independence or helped the cause with money and supplies. Their loyalty garnered little reward. Even before the formal break with Mexico, the General Council of the Republic of Texas prohibited the entry of any more free blacks into Texas under penalty of enslavement. Once they had defeated the Mexican forces, Texas lawmakers permitted only those people of color who had resided in the region since preindependence days to stay. Eventually they informed even those individuals that they must pay five hundred dollars each *and* get permission from the courts to remain in Texas.

The United States finally annexed Texas in 1845. Statehood brought a further weakening of black rights. Free blacks could not vote or hold office. They could not testify in court, and they were subject to harsher penalties than whites if convicted of the same offense. Should a slave owner decide to free a slave, he or she could only do so beyond the boundaries of the state, and the ex-slave could not return to Texas, although Texas law did give a free person the option to re-enslave him- or herself. Not surprisingly, Texas failed to attract many free black settlers.

Texas annexation led to war with Mexico from 1845–1848, which resulted in the United States gaining a vast amount of new territory in the West, where thousands of blacks had already settled. Free blacks had been trickling into California long before the war. Under Mexican rule, a few people of mixed African, Spanish, and Indian descent in California had enjoyed influence unmatched by anything men and women with any discernible trace of African ancestry could aspire to in the United States.

Andreas Pico was a general who fought against the Americans, and his brother, Pio, was the governor of California at the time of the Mexican surrender. However, people of color were also instrumental in wresting control of California from Mexico. William Leidesdorff, a man of African and Danish parentage, arrived in California in 1841. Originally from St. Croix, he made Yerba Buena, today's San Francisco, his base of operations. Leidesdorff was a rancher, a land speculator, a ship-owner and a very successful merchant. Although he took Mexican citizenship, he sided with the Americans. Had he lived longer—he died in 1848—his wealth and political astuteness would have made him a force to reckon with when California achieved statehood.

Leidesdorff died just before the Gold Rush. The stream of Americans, black and white, making for California became a raging torrent once word spread of the discovery of gold at Sutter's Mill. The population soared, and soon California was on the verge of statehood. The constitutional convention of 1849 drafted a document that banned slavery, in large measure because white prospectors had no desire to compete with huge gangs of slaves panning for gold to enrich their masters.

The war with Mexico and the acquisition by the United States of millions of additional square miles of territory led to the same intense debate that had followed the Louisiana Purchase. Politicians and the white public in general had very different notions about whether or not to permit slavery in the new territories. For the supporters of slavery it was a question of fundamental rights—their rights to take their slaves wherever they chose. For the white abolitionist minority it was about the gross injustice of one human being exploiting another. For many whites who opposed the spread of slavery, though, it came down to their determination to keep the West for white people. As Pennsylvania's David Wilmot declared when he tried to push through Congress a piece of legislation that would have prohibited slavery in all the lands the United States had gained from Mexico, he was "plead[ing] the cause of the rights of white freemen." The West was "a rich inheritance" for "the sons of toil, of my own race and own color."[6] Black slaves did not belong in the West, and neither did black "freemen." The truth was that many whites were prepared to argue that black "freemen" had no right to live *anywhere* in the United States. For the nation's free men and women of color, who had hoped to complete what their parents had begun, the era of "manifest destiny" brought both hope and frustration. They could hope for a better future for themselves and their children, but they could not help feeling a growing sense of frustration. By the 1840s, it seemed that freedom and the rights of American citizenship were only for white people.

American Foot Soldiers. On the eve of the British surrender at Yorktown in 1781, a French officer painted this picture of black men and white men serving together in the Continental Army. Some of the black soldiers were already free, while others hoped to win their freedom by enlisting. (Anne S. K. Brown Military Collection, John Hay Library, Brown University)

Portrait of Elizabeth Freeman (Mumbet). In 1781, Elizabeth Freeman and her lawyer, Theodore Sedgwick, won her freedom and helped end slavery in Massachusetts by arguing that the Massachusetts constitution's guarantee of freedom and equality applied to everyone in the state. Sedgwick's daughter-in-law, Susan Ridley Sedgwick, painted this portrait of Freeman thirty years after her landmark case. (Courtesy of the Massachusetts Historical Society)

Benjamin Banneker's Almanac. *Self-taught mathematician and astronomer Benjamin Banneker (1731–1806), the author of a series of well-received almanacs, publicly challenged Thomas Jefferson in print, asking how the framer of the Declaration of Independence could defend slavery and condemn black people as intellectually inferior to whites. (The Library Company of Philadelphia)*

Bethel African Methodist Episcopal Church, Philadelphia. Founded by Methodist preacher Richard Allen in 1794, Bethel eventually became the "mother church" of the African Methodist Episcopal (AME) denomination and a vibrant hub of black community life. (The Library Company of Philadelphia)

PAUL

CAPTAIN

CUFFE

1812.

From a Drawing by JOHN POLE, M. D. of Bristol, E?

Paul Cuffe. New England–born shipowner Paul Cuffe (1759–1817) played a crucial role in promoting the emigration of American free blacks to Africa. He hoped it would give them greater economic opportunities and lead to the abolition of slavery. (Courtesy of the New Bedford Whaling Museum)

Black Sawyers Working in Front of the Bank of Pennsylvania, Philada. The working people in this lively Philadelphia street scene painted around 1811 by German-born artist John Lewis Krimmel were most likely free. However, even though the men were skilled craftsmen, they may not have been able to find steady employment. The nursemaid probably lived in her employers' home rather than with her own family. (Rogers Fund, The Metropolitan Museum of Art. Image source: ART RESOURCE)

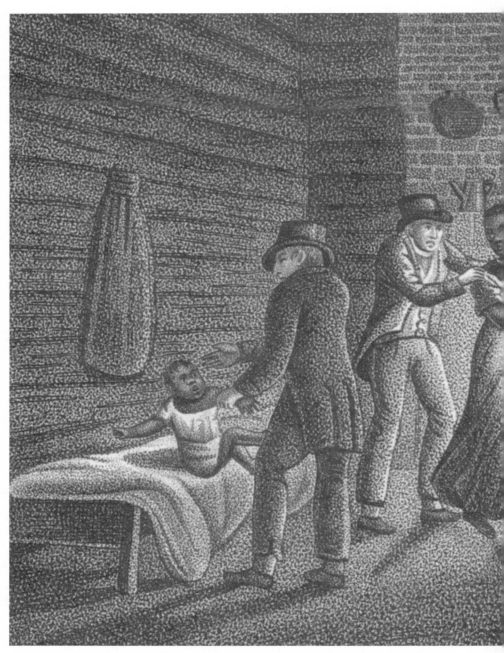

Kidnapping. As this illustration from Joseph Torrey's A Portraiture of Domestic Slavery (Philadelphia, 1817) shows, even in the supposedly free states black people were in danger of being kidnapped and sold into slavery. (The Library Company of Philadelphia)

Black and White Beaux. This refined and elegantly-dressed young couple out for a stroll in New York City belonged to the black middle class that was emerging in a number of communities by 1830. (From Frances Trollope, Domestic Manners of the Americans *[1832], The Library Company of Philadelphia)*

James Forten. Born to free black parents in Philadelphia, James Forten (1766–1842) served on an American privateer during the Revolutionary War while still in his mid-teens and then carved out a career for himself as a successful sail-maker and real estate speculator. He was an outspoken critic of slavery and racial inequality. (Leon Gardiner Collection, Historical Society of Pennsylvania)

WALKER'S

APPEAL,

IN FOUR ARTICLES,

TOGETHER WITH

A PREAMBLE

TO THE

COLORED CITIZENS OF THE WORLD,

BUT IN PARTICULAR, AND VERY EXPRESSLY TO THOSE OF THE

UNITED STATES OF AMERICA.

Written in Boston, in the State of Massachusetts, Sept. 28th, 1829.

Boston:

PUBLISHED BY DAVID WALKER.

1829.

David Walker's Appeal. *David Walker's 1829 pamphlet urged free blacks to insist on equality with whites and told the nation's slaves to demand their freedom. The Appeal outraged the defenders of the racial status quo, and when Walker died in 1830 of tuberculosis it was rumored that he had in fact been murdered.*
(The Library Company of Philadelphia)

Francis Johnson. Francis Johnson (1792–1844) toured extensively in North America and Europe with his band, which was made up entirely of African-American musicians, and composed music for many white upper-class social events. This portrait is by Robert Douglass Jr., a black painter from Philadelphia who struggled to make his own career in the arts. (Ferdinand J. Dreer Collection, Historical Society of Pennsylvania)

CAUTION!!

COLORED PEOPLE

OF BOSTON, ONE & ALL,

You are hereby respectfully CAUTIONED and advised, to avoid conversing with the

Watchmen and Police Officers of Boston,

For since the recent ORDER OF THE MAYOR & ALDERMEN, they are empowered to act as

KIDNAPPERS

AND

Slave Catchers,

And they have already been actually employed in KIDNAPPING, CATCHING, AND KEEPING SLAVES. Therefore, if you value your LIBERTY, and the *Welfare of the Fugitives* among you, *Shun* them in every possible manner, as so many *HOUNDS* on the track of the most unfortunate of your race.

Keep a Sharp Look Out for KIDNAPPERS, and have TOP EYE open.

APRIL 24, 1851.

Caution!! Colored People. The passage of a harsh new Fugitive Slave Law in 1850 made free blacks feel vulnerable. They could be arrested as runaways, denied the chance to prove that they were in fact free, and shipped off to the South. (Photographs and Print Division, Schomburg Center for Research in Black Culture, The New York Public Library, Astor, Lenox and Tilden Foundations)

CHAPTER FIVE

~

"No Rights which the White Man was Bound to Respect"

Black Freedom and Black Citizenship, 1850–1861

The message the new generation of African-American leaders wanted to convey to the entire free black community was that if they hoped to see every slave in the nation liberated and every free person treated as a citizen they must unite. It was one thing to call upon people to rally around the core issue of ending racial oppression. It was quite another, however, to reach a consensus about how best to proceed, or indeed who should speak

Table 5.1   Free Black Population in Selected U.S. Cities, 1790, 1820, and 1850

	1790	1820	1850
Baltimore	323	10,326	25,442
Boston	761	1,687	1,999
Charleston, SC	775	1,475	3,441
Chicago	——	——	323
Cincinnati	——	433	3,237
Louisville, KY	1	93	1,538
Nashville, TN	——	189	511
New Orleans	862	6,237	9,905
New York	1,036	10,368	13,815
Philadelphia	1,805	10,710	17,142
Providence, RI	417	975	1,499
Richmond, VA	265	1,235	2,369
St. Louis	37	196	1,470
Washington, D.C.	——	1,696	8,158

Sources: Federal Population Schedules for the Years 1790, 1820, and 1850; Kimberly S. Hanger, *Bounded Lives, Bounded Places: Free Black Society in Colonial New Orleans, 1769–1803* (Durham: Duke University Press, 1997), 22 (1791 census for Spanish-held New Orleans); www.usgennet.org/usa/mo/county/stlouis/census.htm (accessed May 2, 2013) (1791 census for Spanish-held St. Louis)

for the nation's free black population. By 1850, that population stood at almost 435,000. Free people of color lived in every state of the Union and in every territory. They dwelled on small farms and in great cities. Some were wealthy, while many were desperately poor. Several hundred were slaveholders, while a great many more were ex-slaves. Although most were legally free, a considerable number—we will never know the precise figure—were passing as free. Geography and socioeconomic status divided the free community, and so too did gender. Black women struggled with the "double bond" of race and gender; when they spoke out, some black men were supportive but others dismissed their concerns. Although unity was difficult to achieve across lines of region and class, education and gender, the overwhelming majority of free people were agreed on one central point: things could not remain as they were.

The new decade began ominously for the nation's free people of color. Negotiators in Congress patched together the Compromise of 1850 to try to damp down the fires of sectional discord. California entered the Union as a free state, a move that seemed promising to African Americans who wanted to settle there. The Compromise organized New Mexico and Utah into territories. It resolved a boundary dispute between Texas and New Mexico, and it banned the slave trade in the District of Columbia. Foreign visitors to the nation's capital had been openly critical of the fact that auctioneers were selling off slaves to the highest bidder just blocks away from where congressmen were holding forth on the subject of American liberty. The slave trade ended in the District, although slavery did not, but by far the most controversial provision of the Compromise was the passage of a new Fugitive Slave Law.

Slaveholders had been complaining for decades that the 1793 law was not tough enough. They wanted a law that had "teeth." In 1850 they got it. The new Fugitive Slave Law was broad in its scope and truly terrible in its impact. It made every African American vulnerable to arrest and enslavement. Slave owners or their agents had the power of the federal government behind them. Armed with vague descriptions of the individuals they were hunting, they roamed black neighborhoods in the North and Midwest. The people they seized as fugitives were judged to be so unless they could prove otherwise—but they could not prove otherwise because the law did not allow them to bring forward witnesses to attest to their free status. The fact that the federally-appointed commissioners responsible for determining whether the black man or woman standing before them was a slave or a free person received ten dollars if they ruled in favor of the slave catcher and only five if they found that it was a case of mistaken identity obviously weighed in the decision-making process.

In Boston and elsewhere, black and white antislavery radicals stormed courthouses, harassed slave catchers, and did whatever they could to wrest alleged runaways from the clutches of their captors. If they had to use violence, some were prepared to do so. In at least one instance—in Christiana, Pennsylvania, in 1851—a slave owner paid with his life for attempting to take back his human property. As Frederick Douglass proclaimed, "The only way to make the Fugitive Slave Law a dead letter is to make half a dozen or more dead kidnappers."[1] Black people began to arm themselves and some of them fortified their homes.

The federal government repeatedly intervened to uphold the law. The "rendition" of Anthony Burns in Boston in 1854 took so much manpower and generated so much expense that, humanitarian considerations apart, critics of the slave law insisted that it would have been cheaper if the authorities had simply paid Burns' master for his freedom. Nine "free" states either revamped their personal liberty laws or wrote new ones. Those states might not give black people many rights in their everyday lives, but they were concerned about the implications of the federal law. Tensions escalated as the defenders of slavery demanded that the Supreme Court strike down the state laws.

The 1852 publication of Harriet Beecher Stowe's *Uncle Tom's Cabin* stiffened the resolve of the antislavery forces and brought them new recruits. Some African-American readers were dismayed that Stowe's novel ended with George and Eliza Harris leaving for Liberia. They argued that Stowe should have had this brave young couple stay and fight the slave system, but they appreciated the response *Uncle Tom's Cabin* generated. It brought home to many of Stowe's white readers the evils of slavery and the pernicious nature of the Fugitive Slave Law. However, sympathy for the poor, oppressed slaves in the South did not necessarily change the way whites in the "free" states viewed people of color in general. The body of laws in place in all sections of the nation reinforced to free black people their marginal status, and where the law was silent, majority sentiment often ruled the day. If race riots were less prevalent in the 1850s, racial violence was as commonplace as it had ever been. The mob actions of earlier decades had given way to smaller-scale but no less virulent assaults on black people and black-owned property. An unstable economy only made things worse as whites took out their fears and frustrations on their black neighbors.

Facing an uncertain future, some light-skinned free people tried to redefine themselves in racial terms. Charleston's James Hanscome was one individual who succeeded. Hanscome was the wealthy slave-owning son of a white planter and a free woman of color. Under South Carolina law, the child of a Native-American woman and a white man was considered white, so Hanscome declared that his late mother had been an Indian. He also insisted that he had never paid the discriminatory tax that South Carolina imposed on all free people of color, and hence he never had been "colored." He even produced as a witness the official responsible for collecting the tax. Both men lied. Hanscome *had* paid the tax. Whether his white ally perjured himself out of friendship or because Hanscome had bribed him is open to question, but no one checked, and Hanscome slipped quietly across the racial boundary. What he achieved was hardly unusual. A newspaper in Charleston around the same time that James Hanscome "passed" lamented that "[e]very day" free people stretched the truth and "gained the privileges of white men."[2]

Suspicion of free people increased in many quarters. Even if only a small number of them were able to do what Hanscome had done, many whites saw free blacks as constituting a dangerous and restless element in society. Southern states made vigorous efforts to cut off the flow of recruits into the free community. Manumission became virtually impossible in most slave states after 1850. Courts that had once been fairly liberal in their interpretation of what counted as a "meritorious act" on the part of a slave now adopted a much harsher attitude. And when the laws of a particular state required that newly-emancipated slaves leave immediately or face reenslavement, judges were less likely than they had been to grant waivers. Masters and mistresses who did want to liberate a slave often found that they could not do so. If an owner defied the law rather than trying to maneuver around it, that did not help the slave, who would find him- or herself back in slavery by order of the state. Local authorities in the South began conducting sweeps of particular neighborhoods, taking into custody black people who had been living as free, with or without the connivance of their owners.

Under the circumstances, it is hardly surprising that some free people chose to leave the United States. A new Haitian emigration scheme induced hundreds of men and women to try their luck in the island nation. People of color reevaluated emigration to Liberia. In the 1820s and 1830s, the free community had been intensely critical of the American Colonization Society and had condemned as foolish and misguided anyone who even considered going to Liberia. However, in 1847 Liberia had become an independent republic and it had a black man, Virginia-born merchant John Jenkins Roberts, as its president. That made it much more appealing.

Black men and women left America to seek better opportunities elsewhere. Some, like abolitionist lecturer Sarah Parker Remond and gifted young scholar Jesse Ewing Glasgow, sought in Britain the college education they could not get in the United States. France attracted a number of mixed-raced émigrés from Louisiana. Some people ventured much further afield.

African-American mariners and whalers jumped ship in faraway locations like Hawai'i, while black prospectors joined whites in seeking their fortunes in the gold diggings in Australia.

Opportunity motivated some people, but sheer panic drove others into exile. Reports that slave catchers had arrived in town prompted escaped slaves to head for the Canadian border in droves. In many cases those individuals and their families had been living as free for years, and their neighbors were stunned when they packed up and disappeared overnight. An unknown number who were legally free fled north as well, fearful that the slave catchers might seize *them* and ship *them* off to the South. Whatever prompted free blacks to leave America, black leaders in the 1850s were far less critical of voluntary emigration than those of an earlier generation had been. As Martin R. Delany saw it, black people should turn their backs on a nation that was obviously rejecting them. "We love our country, dearly love her, but she . . . despises us, and bids us begone." He recommended that they move to any country willing to "receive [them] as her adopted children."[3]

Although thousands of free blacks left the United States in the 1850s, the overwhelming majority stayed. Plenty of white people hoped that *they* would go as well because, in their opinion, the nation would be better off without them. Pressure mounted in various parts of the South for a black exodus. Virginia, Maryland, Missouri, and Kentucky earmarked public funds to advance the African colonization scheme. In 1853, the Tennessee legislature announced that henceforth every slave who gained his or her freedom must leave for Liberia. On at least two occasions, South Carolina lawmakers advocated rounding up free people and reducing them to slavery. Some free blacks panicked and fled the state. Others laid low, hoping the storm would soon blow over.

Arkansas lawmakers told free blacks outright that they must leave or lose their liberty. Admittedly, Arkansas's free population was not a large one— it numbered just 608 in 1850—but most free people heeded the warning and left. Virginia twice debated expulsion in the 1850s. North Carolina considered it, as did Maryland. There were rumors of similar moves afoot in Missouri, although ultimately they came to nothing. James Thomas recalled how the authorities in St. Louis had ordered all the free people in the city, some 1,500 individuals, to appear in court and answer questions about who they were, where they lived, and how they supported themselves. The situation in the free states was different in one major respect. Since slavery was dead, black people could not be reduced to chattel once more. They could, however, be made to feel that they counted for very little in other respects.

With prospects so gloomy in the North and the South, some free blacks hoped they might do better in the West. Many hundreds joined the surge of white Forty-Niners into California during the Gold Rush. In common with the majority of the white prospectors, most African Americans stayed even after they realized they were never going to strike it rich in the goldfields. California entered the Union as a free state, and that attracted more black settlers, but being a free state did not qualify California as a haven of peaceful coexistence. Some slave owners defied the law, brought their slaves to California, and tried to keep them. California's fugitive slave law helped them do so because it allowed people who did not reside permanently in the state to own slaves. Slaveholders simply lied about where they lived, and if their slaves ran away they hunted them down and reclaimed them, with the approval of the local courts.

African Americans had to contend with all sorts of legal disabilities in California. They could not vote or testify in court. There was even talk of stopping any more black people coming to California to live. Throughout the 1850s tensions ran high in California over the intertwined issues of slavery and the rights of people of color. Some black Californians decided it was simply not worth trying to change the hearts and minds of white people in the state and left, some to go back East, others to see if they could find a warmer welcome elsewhere in the West. Many more stayed put, however, ready to fight to preserve the rights they had and try to secure for their community the privileges that other Californians enjoyed.

In general, the West and the Southwest extended to black people no more legal rights than they had enjoyed back East. Oregon prohibited African Americans from owning land, making contracts, or suing in the courts. Eventually the state closed its borders to free blacks. Whites in Oregon did not want slaves, and Oregon was technically a free state, but it was hardly free in the sense in which black people understood freedom. When white settlers in the region north of the Columbia River separated from Oregon and formed the Washington territory, African Americans who tried to settle in the new territory encountered just as much hostility as in Oregon. Some of those who simply could not or would not endure the treatment whites meted out to them in the Pacific Northwest moved further north to British Columbia, especially after word spread of the 1858 Fraser Canyon Gold Rush.

Much further south, the territorial legislature of New Mexico (which included Arizona) enacted a ban on the entry of free people of color in 1856. Free blacks, most of them from Arkansas and Missouri, still managed to find their way into New Mexico. The numbers were small—fewer than a hundred by 1860—but the presence of these men and women indicates that at least some African Americans were prepared to brave not only the wilderness but oppressive laws to seek economic independence in the Southwest.

When it came to the Nebraska Territory and a prefiguring of the bloody struggle of the Civil War, free people of color did not fare much better in regard to legal rights than they did elsewhere. The legislation that Illinois Senator Stephen A. Douglas pushed through Congress in 1854 created the Nebraska Territory out of the enormous expanse of land between the Rocky Mountains and the Missouri River and split it in two, creating Nebraska and Kansas. The Kansas-Nebraska Act authorized the settlers themselves to vote on whether or not they wanted slavery.

Nebraska became a free state, and a racially very homogeneous one. White settlers had no need for slavery, and no need for free black people either. By 1860, there were fewer than fifty in the entire state. The first free black settler, Sally Bayne, arrived in 1854 or 1855. More followed. Some took up the trades they had pursued back home. Kentucky native Jeremiah Crump was a barber. He and his wife, Jemima, lived in the fledgling settlement of Omaha with their infant son at the time of the 1860 census. A black shoemaker from New York, Cornelius Bye, lived next door to the Crumps with two white men who worked in the same trade. Other new arrivals gravitated to Nebraska City or forsook town life for farming. While white pioneers in Nebraska may not have been particularly well disposed toward blacks, they did not try to force them out of the state.

Black settlers who went to Kansas in the 1850s quickly discovered that they were in a war zone. Pro- and antislavery forces fought savagely for control of the territory. In 1859, Kansas entered the Union as a "free" state, but not one that accepted blacks as citizens. The 1860 census recorded that there were just 625 people of color living in Kansas, although the actual figure may have been higher because of the numbers of slaves who fled from neighboring Missouri, passed as free in Kansas, and hid from the census-takers.

Many abolitionists thought that if slavery could not spread, maybe it would die. That all changed, however, with a ruling of the nation's highest court. In the 1830s, white army surgeon John Emerson traveled around the Midwest, taking his slaves, Dred and Harriet Scott, with him to places where slavery was illegal, before settling back in Missouri, a slave state. The Scotts did not try to escape, but after Emerson died they went to court and sued their new owner for their freedom on the basis that they had been in free territory and as such were no longer slaves. After a decade, their case eventually wound up in the U.S. Supreme Court. What happened in the case of *Dred Scott vs. Sandford* would determine not only the status of the Scotts but the constitutionality of the Missouri Compromise, which had limited where slavery could exist. Across the nation people watched intently, none more intently than America's free people of color.

In the spring of 1857, the justices overturned the Missouri Compromise by a majority of seven to two. They ruled that the Scotts' residence with their master in the free state of Illinois and then in the supposedly free territory of Wisconsin did not make them free. To many whites outside the South this seemed a harbinger of worse to come. Now slavery could spread into the territories and might even regain a foothold in the "free" states. To the free black community the ruling was infinitely worse. It struck at their sense of themselves as Americans because the court had essentially declared that African Americans, regardless of whether they were enslaved or free, had no rights that whites had to respect. They were not citizens, they never had been citizens, and they never would be, according to the justices. Wealth, education, respectability—nothing would alter it.

At this point, some free people who had previously been undecided about emigrating concluded that it was time to heed Martin R. Delany's advice and leave. They had not rejected America. America had rejected them. Other people began organizing ad hoc military units for the great conflict they believed was surely coming over the issue of black freedom. This was an era of growing militancy within at least certain segments of the free community. African Americans were far from passive observers as the nation came apart at the seams. They held three national conventions during the 1850s and no fewer than twenty state conventions. The *Dred Scott* decision only strengthened the resolve of many free people to rally in defense of their rights. They petitioned their state and local governments, and in some instances they took their complaints to Congress. In the handful of states where they could vote, they did so, although only after asking searching questions about where a particular candidate stood on the cause of black freedom.

Free people repeatedly put their lives on the line. Women and men participated in slave rescues and aided fugitive slaves in many ways. As far as they were concerned, it was irrelevant that they themselves were free. The slaves' cause was their cause. The fact that the Supreme Court had struck down the Missouri Compromise and, at least by implication, given slaveholders the right to take their slaves into any state or territory, endangered the liberty of all black people across the nation. With the foreign slave trade illegal, opening new lands for slavery boosted the price of slaves, and hence the profits unscrupulous whites could make from kidnapping free people. Many free blacks saw slavery and freedom as two sides of the same coin, and they became more outspoken and more militant. Five black men, all but one of them legally free, fought alongside John Brown in the raid on the arsenal at Harpers Ferry in 1859, trying to get weapons to free slaves. If some black leaders like Frederick Douglass ultimately decided that they would not join Brown and his men, it was not because they wanted to focus on securing their own rights while ignoring the plight of the enslaved. It was simply that they did not think Brown's plan would succeed.

That, of course, begged the question of what Douglass and other black leaders thought *would* succeed. Some put their faith in the political process, but the occupants of the White House in the 1850s were either indifferent or downright hostile to black freedom, and the election of 1860 did not inspire much hope for change. None of the candidates supported abolition or seemed willing to address the status of the nation's free people. Republican nominee Abraham Lincoln had gone the furthest in his speeches, but hardly far enough. While he had declared his personal distaste for slavery, he had also insisted that he was not "in favor of bringing about in any way the social and political equality of the white and black race."[4]

As most of the slaveholding states seceded on the eve of Lincoln's inauguration and the new president called for troops to put down the rebellion, free men of color stepped forward. The recruiters informed them that their services were not needed and federal law forbade them to enlist anyway. The nation's free people of color watched and waited, certain only of two things: this was a war about slavery, whatever the politicians said about states' rights, and sooner or later the United States would have to address what freedom meant for black people. Lincoln had said the nation could not endure half-slave and half-free. He had been speaking in political terms. They interpreted "half-free" very differently. Half-free was what *they* were, and it was what four million slaves were likely to be if black freedom continued to mean an inferior brand of freedom. As they saw it, and as generations of black men and women before them had seen it, half-free was not free enough. Black people had lived in the "borderlands" between slavery and true freedom for far too long. It was time for that to change.

In 1860, the United States census recorded the nation's free black population at just under half a million and its slave population at almost four million. The census-takers had followed their instructions and listed the two segments of black society not on different pages of the census but in entirely different documents. "Free persons of color" belonged on the population schedules along with white people. Slaves belonged on the "slave schedules." They were not listed by their own names but by age, gender, and complexion, under the names of their owners. In 1860, they were "property," not persons.

By the time the United States conducted its next census, slavery was dead. Every black man, woman, and child was now a person, and the nation had almost five million black people living within its borders. All black people were free, although the nation was still coming to terms with what that meant. What it often meant at the state and local levels was that whites revisited the old laws that had regulated the lives of "free persons of color" during the era of slavery. If all black people were now free, then they must all be subject to those same laws. And where the laws were imprecise or insufficient, then the assumptions and attitudes that had governed the interactions between whites and free blacks must govern them still.

Freedom was not without a deeper meaning for black people in the United States. It could not possibly be. Generations of black men and women had endured so much to achieve it. What they had hoped for, though, was that freedom and equality would eventually become one and the same. That had not happened in colonial days. It had not happened as the colonies declared their independence from Britain and committed themselves to "life, liberty and the pursuit of happiness." It had not happened in the years since independence. Somehow, liberty had never translated into "the pursuit of happiness" for the nation's free people of color. They had been free, but they had not been citizens. When the United States Supreme Court ruled in the *Dred Scott* case that they were not and never had been citizens, that was true—by and large. The justices had also predicted, though, that black people would never be citizens and that freedom would make no difference to their status. The decades after Emancipation would put that to the test. All black people, not just a percentage of the black population, were free. Half-free or fully free, stranded somewhere between "slave" and "citizen"—that had been the reality for free black people for centuries. Now that all were free, it would become the measure of the nation's commitment to liberty to determine whether a separate "black freedom" would disappear and give way simply to freedom for all.

~

Documents

Laws on Black Freedom in Colonial Virginia and Massachusetts

The English colonies of Virginia and Massachusetts both recognized slavery and placed limitations on black freedom, but they did so in rather different ways. In its 1641 "Body of Liberties" Massachusetts sanctioned the enslavement of all "lawful captives taken in just warres, and such strangers as willingly sell themselves or are sold to us." What happened in Virginia, though, was a step-by-step defining of who was and was not free. By the 1660s, Virginia law declared, among other things, that a child inherited the status of his or her mother (1662) and that slaves who became Christians were still slaves (1667). In neither colony did the authorities want the slaves to get their freedom. Virginia lawmakers took action in 1691 by approving "An Act for suppressing outlying slaves." In 1703, Massachusetts passed "An Act Relating to Molato and Negro Slaves." Both penalized owners who emancipated their slaves, and Virginia punished the newly-freed slaves for becoming free by forcing them into exile.

Virginia

Whereas some doubts have arisen whether children got by any Englishman upon a Negro woman should be slave or free, be it therefore enacted and declared . . . that all children born in this country shall be held bond or free only according to the condition of the mother.

Whereas some doubts have arisen whether children that are slaves by birth, and by the Charity and piety of their owners made partakers of the blessed sacrament of baptism, should by virtue of their baptism be made free, it is enacted and declared . . . that the conferring of baptism does not alter the condition of the person as to his bondage or freedom.

And forasmuch as great inconveniences may happen to this country by the setting of negroes and mulattoes free, by their either entertaining negro slaves from their masters' service, or receiving stolen goods, or being grown old bringing a charge upon the country; for prevention thereof . . . it is hereby enacted, That no negro or mulatto be . . . set free by any person or persons whatsoever, unless such person or persons, their heirs, executors or administrators pay for the transportation of such negro or negroes out of the country within six months after . . . setting them free.

Source: William Waller Hening, comp., *The Statutes at Large, Being a Collection of all the Laws of Virginia from the First Session of the Legislature in the Year 1619* (Richmond: R. & W. & G. Bartow, 1819–23), vol. 2, pp. 170, 260; vol. 3, p. 88.

Massachusetts

Whereas great charge[s] and inconveniences have arisen to divers towns and places, by the releasing and setting at liberty [of] molato [sic] and negro slaves; for prevention whereof for the future,—Be it declared and enacted by His Excellency the Governour [sic], Council and Representatives in General Court assembled, and by the authority of the same,

[Sect. 1.] That no molato or negro slave shall hereafter be . . . set free, until sufficient security be given to the treasurer of the town or place where such person dwells, in a valuable sum, not less than fifty pounds, to . . . indempnify [sic] the town or place from all charge for or about such molato or negro, to be . . . set at liberty, in case he or she by sickness, lameness, or otherwise, be rendered uncapable [sic] to support him- or herself.

Source: *The Acts and Resolves, Public and Private, of the Province of Massachusetts Bay* (Boston: Wright and Potter, Printers to the State, 1869), vol. 1, p. 519.

～

Passing as Free (1736–1773)

These notices for the return of runaway slaves reveal more than the people who posted them ever intended. The individual slave owners simply wanted their "property" back. What the advertisements tell us, though, is that a small but

growing free black community existed by the early eighteenth century in virtually every colony, that some slaves hoped to take advantage of that fact and pass as free, and that free people often helped friends and family members who were still enslaved. They also speak to punishments meted out, physical disabilities overcome, skills acquired, and careful preparations put into plotting escapes.

THIS is to forewarn all Persons of entertaining the blind Negro called America, well known about Philadelphia, who is not free as he sometimes pretends to be, but belongs to William Morgan, in Second-Street.

Source: *Pennsylvania Gazette*, March 18, 1736

Run-away on Friday Afternoon . . . a likely Negro Man named Jacob, belonging to George Wray, at Albany; the said Negro is about 24 Years old . . . has a Scar on the right Side of his Forehead, one on his left Temple . . . and another on the Crown of his Head . . . a lump on each shoulder by being flogg'd some Time past . . . speaks good English, some French, and a little Spanish. . . . [He is] of an insinuating Address, very apt to feign plausible Stories, and may perhaps call himself a free Negro. . . . He had on when he went away, a Blanket Coat, Green Leggings and Moccasins, Buckskin Breeches and a red Worsted Cap. It is supposed he had with him, a black and white spotted Dog, answering to the Name of Venture.

Source: *New York Mercury*, March 5, 1764

Run away from my plantation on Indian Land . . . a MULATTO FELLOW called VIRGINIA JOHN. . . . He is a very artful fellow, and may endeavor to pass himself for a free mulatto, and assumes different names as it suits him. . . . Masters of vessels are desired to take notice . . . as he may attempt to impose on them by his artfulness, in order to get off from this province.

Source: *Georgia Gazette*, November 22, 1764

Sussex County, on [the] Delaware, Three Run Mills
Ran away . . . a Mulatto Slave, named HARRY, about 40 years of age. . . . He was bred a miller, and understands very well how to manufacture flour, and can invoice the same; is much given to strong drink, and playing on the violin; understands the carpenter's and mill-wright's business middling well. . . . [T]he said fellow has a free Mulatto wife, named Peg, and two children. I expect they will endeavor to get together . . . [and] get to the province of New-Jersey. It is imagined said Mulatto has a pass.

Source: *Pennsylvania Chronicle*, June 27–July 4, 1768

Ran away from the Subscriber, on Friday the 9th day of July . . . a Mulatto Woman Slave named *Violetas*, aged about 32 Years, of short Stature. . . . She had with her when she went away a Chintz Gown . . . a Couple of Quilts . . . two Pair of Shoes, and divers other Things—If any Person shall inform where she is, that her Master may have her again, they shall be well rewarded. . . . N.B. It is suspected she is in Company with one *Henry Traveller*, a free Negro.

Bridgewater, July 12, 1773,

ABIA KEITH

Source: *Boston Evening Post*, July 19, 1773

∽

Free Black People in Colonial Pennsylvania and Rhode Island (1751–1770)

Slavery flourished in the North in the colonial era just as it did in the South, and it flourished in urban centers as well as in the countryside. Much to the annoyance of white people, though, at least some slaves managed to gain their freedom. Local lawmakers responded to complaints about the presence and the activities of free blacks. To begin with, whites insisted that there were simply too many of them. In Philadelphia by 1751, the date of the first law quoted here, there were perhaps 200, compared to several thousand slaves. In the entire colony of Rhode Island by 1770 there were not very many more. However, numbers really did not matter. Whites persisted in regarding free blacks collectively as "an idle, slothful people," and they demanded action to keep them firmly under control. If they could not re-enslave them—and binding them out came very close to re-enslavement— whites wanted free blacks to be told very firmly what they could and could not do. The Pennsylvania law also tried to restrict the further growth of the free black community by making it prohibitively expensive for an owner to manumit a slave.

As frequent Complaints have been lately made to the Magistrates of the City of Philadelphia, that Negroes, and other Blacks, either Free, or under Pretence of Freedom, have . . . settled in the City . . . and have taken Houses, Rooms, and Cellars, for their Habitations, where great disorders often happen, especially in the Night time; and Servants, Slaves, and other idle and vagrant Persons are entertained [and] corrupted. . . . And whereas 'tis found by Experience, that free Negroes are an idle, slothful People; and often prove burthensome to the Neighbourhood, and afford ill Examples to other Negroes: Therefore be it enacted . . . That if any Master or Mistress shall . . . set free any Negroe [sic], he or she shall enter into Recognizance . . . with sufficient Sureties, in the Sum of *Thirty Pounds*, to secure and indemnify the City, Township or County where he resides, from any Charge or Incumbrance they may bring upon the same . . . [and] until such Recognizance be given, such Negroes shall not be deemed free . . . [And] if any free Negroe, fit and able to work, shall neglect so to do, and loiter or misspend his or her Time, or wander from Place to Place, any two Magistrates . . . are hereby impowered and required to bind out to Service such Negroe from Year to Year.

Source: *Pennsylvania Gazette*, March 5, 1751

Whereas it often happens, that free Negroes and Mulattoes keep very disorderly Houses, and entice the Slaves in this Colony to spend much Time and Money in Gaming, Drinking, &c. which they cannot possibly do without robbing their Masters and others . . . Be it therefore Enacted . . . That upon Complaint being made to any Town Council in this Colony, of any free Negro, or Mulatto, who shall keep a disorderly House, or entertain any Slave or Slaves, at unreasonable Hours, or in an extravagant Manner . . . such Town Council be . . . empowered to examine into the Matter, and if they find such free Negro or Mulatto guilty . . . they may . . . break up from House-Keeping such free Negro or Mulatto . . . and bind them as Servants for a Term of Time . . . and . . . commit them to the Work-House until suitable Places can be had for them.

Source: *Providence Gazette*, September 1–8, 1770

～

Free People of Color in the South Carolina Press (1760–1771)

By 1710, blacks outnumbered whites in South Carolina. Most were slaves, but not all were. White South Carolinians regarded free blacks as a class with intense suspicion, as the first notice clearly shows. Poorer whites feared economic competition, and whites of all classes worried that free people would conspire with the slaves and help foment rebellions. However, despite the many legal restrictions they faced and the hostility they encountered from all segments of the white community, individual men and women of color in South Carolina did have opportunities to make money and accumulate property (including slaves). Most importantly of all, they could marry and establish families. We do not know why the Peronneaus' marriage broke up, but Richard Peronneau did what any colonial-era husband would do: he declared publicly that he was no longer financially responsible for his wife. A white husband would have done exactly the same thing.

The Presentments of the Grand Jury for the Body of this Province . . .
We present as a grievance, the evil custom of giving negroes their freedom; and the want of a law to oblige every free negro to wear a badge with their names thereon, by which they may be known . . . We present as a grievance, so many idle negro wenches, selling dry goods, cakes, rice, &c. in the markets, which hinder a great many poor people from getting bread . . . We present as a grievance, the number of small licensed tippling houses, who sell spirituous liquors to sailors and negroes . . .

Source: *South Carolina Gazette*, February 1, 1768

In November next I shall want an OVERSEER, a single man who . . . can be properly recommended; also a free negro or mulatto woman, who understands [running] a dairy, [the] raising of poultry, and [the] cutting out and making [of] negro cloathes [*sic*], will meet with suitable encouragement.

Source: *South Carolina Gazette*, August 30, 1760

All Persons indebted to Charles Cordes (Free Negro) deceased, are desired to make immediate payment to the Subscriber; and those to whom the said Charles Cordes was indebted, are desired to make known their Demands to JOHN GOUGH, *Administrator*.

Source: *South Carolina Gazette*, September 20, 1770

To be SOLD at the Vendue-House in Charles-Town, on TUESDAY, the 23rd of October, Instant; THREE NEGROES, late the Property of A Free Negro Wench, deceased, viz.—A young FELLOW, who is a Carpenter by Trade, and is said to be a good Workman—a likely LAD, about 16 Years of Age—and a WENCH.

Source: *South Carolina Gazette & Country Journal*, October 9, 1770

Charles-Town, September 27, 1771
RICHARD PERONNEAU, a free Negro Carpenter . . . forewarns all persons, not to trust his wife, a free wench named Nancy, a mulatto, on his account, as he is determined not to pay any debts of her contracting from the date hereof, as she has eloped from him.

Source: *South Carolina Gazette*, October 3, 1771

~

Petitioning for Freedom in New Hampshire (1779)

In the autumn of 1779, Nero Brewster and nineteen other slaves in Portsmouth, New Hampshire, petitioned the state legislature. They were careful to explain that they were not condemning their masters but rather the fundamental injustice of slavery. They pledged that if they were freed they would be exemplary citizens and would help in the fight to achieve independence from Britain. Desperate for manpower, New Hampshire did eventually offer bounties to slave owners who manumitted their slaves so that they could serve in the army. In 1783, the new state constitution declared that "all men are born equal and independent." Not until 1857 did New Hampshire actually pass an abolition law, but by then all of the Granite State's black residents were free, although they seldom enjoyed the "equality of freemen" that Brewster and his friends had hoped to secure for themselves and their descendants.

We know we ought to be free agents! [W]e feel the dignity of human nature! [W]e feel the passions and desires of men, tho' checked by the rod of slavery! [W]e feel a just equality! [W]e know that the God of Nature made us free! . . . Should the Humanity and Benevolence of this Honorable Assembly restore us to that State of Liberty of which we have been so long deprived . . . those who are our present Masters will not be Sufferers by our Liberation, as we have most of us spent our whole Strength, and the Prime of our Lives in their Service; And as Freedom inspires a noble Confidence, and gives the Mind an Emulation to vie in the noblest efforts of Enterprise, and as Justice and Humanity are the results of your Deliberations; we fondly hope that the Eye of Pity and the Heart of Justice may Commiserate our Situation and put us upon the Equality of Freemen and give us an Opportunity of evincing to the World our Love of Freedom by exerting ourselves in her Cause, in opposing the Efforts of Tyranny and Oppression over the Country in which we ourselves have been so long injuriously enslaved.

Therefore, your humble slaves most devoutly pray, for the sake of injured liberty, for the sake of justice, humanity, and the rights of mankind; for the honor of religion, and by all that is dear, that your honors would graciously interpose on our behalf . . . [so that] we may regain our liberty . . . and that the name of SLAVE may no more be heard in a land gloriously contending for the sweets of freedom.

Portsmouth, Nov. 12, 1779

Source: *New Hampshire Gazette*, July 15, 1780

～

Richard Allen Buys his Freedom (1780)

On January 25, 1780, in Delaware, a young enslaved man identified simply as "Richard" negotiated to buy his freedom from white farmer Stokeley Sturgis. "Richard" is better known to history as Richard Allen (1760–1831), the founder of the African Methodist Episcopal (AME) church. In his autobiography Allen remembered Sturgis as "a kind, affectionate and tender-hearted master" who had trusted him and allowed him to leave the farm to look for work. Allen took work wherever he could find it, earned the price of his freedom, and paid Sturgis in full two years ahead of time.

I Stokeley Sturgis of Kent County in the Delaware State for the Consideration of the Sum of Sixty Pounds (Old Rates) . . . to be paid at five yearly payments of Twelve pounds [per] year at or upon the Second Day of February in every year the first payment to be made on the Second Day of February which shall be in the year of our Lord One Thousand Seven hundred & Eighty One. Otherwise the yearly Sum of Four hundred Dollars Continental Currency to be paid yearly for the Term of five years as aforesaid by Richard Negro . . . the Choice in Which Currency the payments are to be made always to be at the Option of the Negro and if the said Negro Chuses to pay it in Continental Currency . . . he must Work Two Days Wages free in Harvest Time for the said Stokeley Sturgis . . . [and] upon the just payment thereof I Do hereby . . . Release and for Ever Discharge and set at full Liberty the said Negro Man named Richard . . . and further I Do hereby fully Trust and Impower him to Hire[,] Deal and Transact for himself with any person Whatsoever from the Second Day of February next.

Source: Pennsylvania Abolition Society Manuscripts, Historical Society of Pennsylvania

～

Benjamin Banneker's Challenge to Thomas Jefferson (1791)

In 1791, a free black farmer in Maryland, Benjamin Banneker (1731–1806), wrote an extraordinary letter to Secretary of State Thomas Jefferson to ask how the author of the Declaration of Independence could defend slavery. Banneker was never enslaved. His grandmother was a white indentured servant and he derived his freedom from her, but he was painfully aware of the condition of the majority of black people. Banneker also took Jefferson to task for maintaining that blacks lacked the mental capacity of whites. He had had only a limited education. His grandmother had taught him to read and write, and he had briefly attended a Quaker school near his family's farm. However, he had demonstrated an aptitude for mathematics early in life, and with the loan of books and a telescope from a white acquaintance he had mastered astronomy. When he wrote Jefferson, he had just returned home after helping to survey the site of the nation's new capital and he was about to publish the first of his almanacs. Based on astronomical observations and complex mathematical calculations, the almanac, a manuscript copy of which he sent to Jefferson along with his letter, constituted in itself a refutation of black intellectual inferiority.

I suppose it is a truth too well attested to you, to need a proof here, that we are a race of beings, who have long labored under the abuse and censure of the world; that we have long been looked upon with an eye of contempt; and that we have long been considered rather as brutish than human, and scarcely capable of mental endowments . . .

I freely and cheerfully acknowledge, that I am of the African race, and in that color which is natural to them of the deepest dye; and . . . I am not under that state of . . . inhuman captivity, to which too many of my brethren are doomed, but that I have abundantly tasted of the fruition of those blessings, which proceed from that free and unequalled liberty with which you are favored.

Sir, suffer me to recall to your mind, that time, in which the arms and tyranny of the British crown were exerted . . . to reduce you to a state of servitude . . . This, Sir, was a time when you clearly saw into the injustice of a state of slavery . . . but, Sir, how pitiable is it to reflect, that although you were so fully convinced of the benevolence of the Father of Mankind, and of his equal and impartial distribution of these rights and privileges . . . you should at the same time counteract his mercies, in detaining by fraud and violence so numerous a part of my brethren, under groaning captivity and cruel oppression, that you should at the same time be found guilty of that most criminal act, which you professedly detested in others, with respect to yourselves.

I suppose that your knowledge of the situation of my brethren, is too extensive to need a recital here; neither shall I presume to prescribe methods by which they may be relieved, otherwise than by recommending to you and all others, to wean yourselves from those narrow prejudices which you have imbibed with respect to them, and as Job proposed to his friends, "put your soul in their souls' stead;" thus shall your hearts be enlarged with kindness and benevolence towards them; and thus shall you need neither the direction of myself or others, in what manner to proceed herein.

Source: *Copy of a Letter from Benjamin Banneker, to the Secretary of State, with his Answer* (Philadelphia: Daniel Lawrence, 1792), 3–4, 6–9.

～

African Americans Petition Congress (1799)

In December 1799, Absalom Jones and seventy-three other free black Philadelphians petitioned Congress (then meeting in Philadelphia) on behalf of the entire black community of the United States. For free people they asked for laws to prevent kidnapping and forced re-enslavement. For the slaves they asked for a federal gradual abolition law. Members of Congress were outraged. With the Haitian revolution fresh in their minds, they feared that if they accepted and discussed the petition it would encourage blacks to become even bolder and demand equality with whites. Black men might even imagine that they should be able to vote and run for office. Only one member, Massachusetts representative George Thacher, argued in favor of the petitioners, saying that they had used "decent" and "respectful" language and they had as much right as other Americans to ask Congress to consider what they had to say.

To the President, Senate, and House of Representatives.
The Petition of the People of Colour, free men, within the City and Suburbs of Philadelphia, humbly sheweth,

That, thankful to God, our Creator, and to the Government under which we live, for the . . . enjoyment of our natural right to liberty, and the protection of our persons and property, from the oppression and violence which so great a number of like colour and national descent are subject to, we feel ourselves bound . . . to lead honest and peaceable lives . . . yet while we feel impressed with grateful sensations for the Providential favor we ourselves enjoy, we cannot be insensible of the condition of our afflicted brethren, suffering . . . in different parts of these states; but deeply sympathizing with them, are incited by a sense of social duty, and humbly conceive ourselves authorized to address and petition you on their behalf . . . We do not ask for an immediate emancipation of all . . . yet, humbly desire you may exert every means in your power to undo the heavy burdens, and prepare the way for the oppressed to go free, that every yoke may be broken . . . [W]e beseech, that as we are men, we may be admitted to partake of the liberties and unalienable rights . . . held forth [in the Declaration of Independence and the Constitution]; firmly believing that the extending of justice and equity to all classes would be a means of drawing down the blessing of Heaven upon this land, for the peace and prosperity of which, and the real happiness of every member of the community, we fervently pray.

Source: John Parrish, *Remarks on the Slavery of the Black People; Addressed to the Citizens of the United States, Particularly to those who are in Legislative or Executive Stations in the General or State Governments; and also to Such Individuals as Hold Them in Bondage* (Philadelphia: Kimber, Conrad & Co., 1806), 49–51.

⌒

Free People of Color in New Orleans React to the Louisiana Purchase (1804)

Free people of color in and around New Orleans had good reason to fear that the rights they had enjoyed under French and Spanish rule would be cut back after the United States took control of the Louisiana Territory. The members of the elite officer corps of the "colored" militia units were especially worried. They knew that the American authorities regarded armed black men as dangerous and inherently untrustworthy, regardless of their free or slave status. They hastened to assure the new territorial governor, William C. C. Claiborne, that whenever he needed their services he could call upon them and they would be only too happy to prove their loyalty to their new country. The true test of their devotion came a decade later when they helped Andrew Jackson defeat the British in the epic Battle of New Orleans.

To his Excellency, William C. C. Claiborne, Governor General and Intendant of Louisiana.

We, the subscribers, free citizens of Louisiana, beg leave to approach your Excellency with sentiments of respect and esteem, and sincere attachment to the government of the United States.

We are natives of this province, and our dearest interests are connected with its welfare. We therefore feel a lively joy that the sovereignty of the country is at length united with that of the American Republic. We are duly sensible that our personal and political freedom is thereby assured to us forever, and are also impressed with the fullest confidence in the justice and liberality of the government towards every class of citizens which they have taken under their protection.

We [were] employed in the military service of the late governor, and we hope we may be permitted to say, that our conduct in that service has ever been distinguished by a ready attention to the duties required of us. Should we be in like manner honored by the American government, to which every principle of interest as well as affection attaches us, permit us to assure your excellency that we shall serve with fidelity and zeal. We therefore respectfully offer our services to the government as a corps of volunteers, agreeably to any arrangement which may be thought expedient.

Source: *Republican Star* (Maryland), March 20, 1804

~

Black Voting Rights in New York (1810)

Free men of color in New York who owned property and paid taxes expected to be able to cast their votes on election day, and they generally voted for Federalist candidates. It had not escaped their attention that Federalists tended to favor the abolition of slavery in New York and often championed the rights of African Americans, free and enslaved. In 1821, New York would disfranchise all but the wealthiest black men, while giving the vote to poorer white men, but in 1810, when they held an election rally at the appropriately-named Liberty Hall, black New Yorkers were still optimistic about the future and still firmly in the Federalist camp. New York's Democratic Republicans criticized them as naive and misguided, but they replied that they were astute enough to know who their friends were.

At a very numerous and respectable meeting of the free people of colour, held . . . on Saturday evening, April 21, at Liberty Hall, for the purpose of taking into consideration, and of approving of those Candidates that [were] nominated by the Federal Committee . . .

Resolved unanimously, That as free People of Colour, in a Land of Liberty, we claim the privilege, to assemble in a peaceable manner, especially on an occasion so important as the present. . . .

Resolved unanimously, That . . . we are determined to support the Federalist Ticket, fully convinced that from the American Independence the Constitution of these U. States was Federal, and approved of by Washington, the Saviour of our Country, who was first in war and first in peace.

Resolved unanimously, That we owe our gratitude to the Present Corporation of the City of N. York—that we will use all our exertions in behalf of the Federal Ticket, trusting that if Federal men are elevated to the highest offices in the government we shall enjoy the blessings of Liberty and Justice.

Source: *New York Spectator*, April 25, 1810

~

African-American Cultural and Religious Life in Baltimore (1810)

Although slavery was legal in Maryland, Baltimore had one of the largest free black communities in the nation. The wave of emancipations that had taken place across the Upper South in the 1780s, combined with the economic opportunities that Baltimore offered to black migrants, resulted in a free population that numbered almost 4,000 by 1810. However, numbers did not translate into social equality. It would have been unthinkable, for instance, to have asked whites and blacks to sit together, or even enter a building by the same door. On this occasion, black community leaders were eager to display the talents of their young people, raise funds for a new church, and convince upper-class whites that they, too, were law-abiding citizens who valued education and religion.

There will be an exhibition of the African School on Tuesday night next, in the African Church, in Sharp-street. The performance will commence with singing and prayer, after which the Constitution of the Baltimore African Library Society for Mutual Relief will be read . . . and 5 appropriate speeches spoken by 5 of the pupils. Next, a collection will be made in order to defray the expences [sic] of the night, and the surplus (if any) shall be for the purpose of aiding the Trustees of said Church in lessening the debt that is still due on the African Church recently purchased in Old Town. After which, the whole will be concluded with singing and prayer.

Seats will be reserved in the lower part of the house, for the white gentlemen and ladies that may be disposed to attend, who will be admitted in at the side door without tickets.

Sources: *Federal Gazette* (Baltimore) July 16, 1810

~

Protesting Discriminatory Legislation in Pennsylvania (1813)

In 1813, Pennsylvania lawmakers drafted a new law that would have required all black residents to register with the authorities and carry "free papers," just as their counterparts in many southern states had to do. Anyone who failed to register would be subject to arrest and prosecution. The law would also have stopped any more free blacks entering the state. Freeborn black businessman James Forten (1766–1842) begged lawmakers to reconsider. Forten was a veteran of the Revolutionary War. He had heard the Declaration of Independence read in public for the first time, and he considered himself well qualified to instruct lawmakers on the true meaning of "life, liberty and the pursuit of happiness." Ultimately, the Pennsylvania legislature did not pass the proposed law. It was not Forten's pamphlet that influenced lawmakers. It was the wartime crisis the state was facing. The need to defend Pennsylvania against a possible British attack took precedence over every other issue.

Many of our ancestors were brought here more than one hundred years ago; many of our fathers, many of ourselves, have fought and bled for the Independence of our country. . . . Has the God who made the white man and the black, left any record declaring us a different species?

Are not men of colour sufficiently degraded? Why then increase their degradation? . . . There are men among us of reputation and property, as good citizens as any men can be, and who, for their property, pay as heavy taxes as any citizens are compelled to pay. . . . The villainous part of the community, of all colours, we wish to see punished. . . . Enact laws to punish them severely, but do not let them operate against the innocent as well as the guilty.

By the third section of this bill . . . police officers are authorized to apprehend any black, whether a vagrant or a man of reputable character, who cannot produce a Certificate that he has been registered. He is to be arrayed [arraigned] before a justice, who is thereupon to commit him to prison!—The jailor is to advertise a Freeman, and at the expiration of six months, if no owner appear . . . he is to be exposed to sale, and if not sold to be confined at hard labour for seven years!!—Man of feeling, read this! . . . The Constable, whose antipathy generally against the black is very great, will take every opportunity of hurting his feelings!—Perhaps, he sees him at a distance, and having a mind to raise the boys in hue and cry against him, exclaims, "Halloa! Stop the Negro!" The boys, delighting in the sport, immediately begin to hunt him, and immediately from a hundred tongues, is heard the cry—"Hoa, Negro, where is your Certificate!" —Can any thing be conceived more degrading to humanity!—Can any thing be done more shocking to the principles of Civil Liberty! A person arriving from another state, ignorant . . . of such a law, may fall a victim to its cruel oppression. But he is to be advertised, and if no owner appear—How can an owner appear for a man who is free and belongs to no one!—If no owner appear, he is exposed for sale! . . . My God, what a situation is his. Search the legends of tyranny and find no precedent . . . It stands alone. It has been left for Pennsylvania, to raise her ponderous arm against the liberties of the black whose greatest boast has been, that he resided in a State where Civil Liberty, and sacred Justice were administered alike to all . . .

The fifth section of this bill is also peculiarly hard, inasmuch as it prevents freemen from living where they please.—Pennsylvania has always been a refuge from slavery, and to this state the Southern black, when freed, has flown for safety. Why does he this! When masters in many of the Southern states . . . free a particular black, unless the Black leaves the state in so many hours, any person resident of the said state, can have him arrested and again sold to Slavery:—The hunted black is obliged to flee, or remain and be again a Slave. . . . Where shall he go? . . . Is there no spot on earth that will protect him! Against their inclination, his ancestors were forced from their homes by traders in human flesh, and even under such circumstances, the wretched offspring are denied the protection you afford to brutes . . .

Source: *Letters from a Man of Colour, on a Late Bill before the Senate of Pennsylvania* (Philadelphia, 1813)

~

Protesting African Colonization (1817)

The influential white men who came together in Washington, D.C. in December 1816 to found the American Colonization Society emphasized their concern for the nation's entire black population, free and enslaved. Some hoped that slavery would soon be abolished and they saw the colonization of free blacks as a step toward achieving that goal, while others supported the slave system and thought that free blacks should be shipped off to Africa before they inspired the slaves to rebel. Abolitionists or defenders of slavery, they found the idea of the United States becoming a racially inclusive nation with freedom and equality for all of its people totally unacceptable. While the ACS's founders spoke of colonizing somewhere in Africa only those free blacks who wanted to leave America, panic set in once the scheme was reported in the press. Black people throughout the North and Upper

South feared that the ACS's true goal was to round them up and deport them. Black Philadelphians were among the first to voice their opposition.

PHILADELPHIA, Jan. 1817

At a numerous meeting of the People of Colour, convened at Bethel Church, to take into consideration the propriety of remonstrating against the contemplated measure, that is to exile us from the land of our nativity; JAMES FORTEN was called to the chair, and RUSSEL PARROTT, secretary. The intent of the meeting, having been stated by the Chairman, the following Resolutions were adopted, without one dissenting voice.

WHEREAS our ancestors (not of choice) were the first cultivators of the wilds of America, we their descendants feel ourselves entitled to participate in the blessings of her luxuriant soil, which their blood and sweat manured; and that any measures, having a tendency to banish us from her bosom, would not only be cruel, but in direct violation of those principles, which have been the boast of the republic.

Resolved, that we view with deep abhorrence the unmerited stigma attempted to be cast upon the reputation of the free People of Colour, by the promoters of this measure, "that they are a dangerous and useless part of the community" . . .

Resolved, that we never will separate ourselves voluntarily from the slave population in this country; they are our brethren by the ties of consanguinity, of suffering, and of wrongs; and we feel that there is more virtue in suffering privations with them, than fancied advantages for a season.

Source: *American Watchman* (Wilmington, Delaware), September 20, 1817

～

Schooling Black Children in the Nation's Capital (1818)

William Costin and the other free men of color who organized Washington's Resolute Beneficial Society knew they had to be cautious. In the heart of a slave-holding community they were proposing to open a school for free black children and for slaves whose owners were prepared to enroll them. They were well aware that many whites feared the consequences of educating blacks. Give free blacks the chance to learn to read and write, so the argument went, and they would teach the slaves. Actually send slaves to school and you were asking for trouble. Costin and his friends assured slaveholders that they and the teacher they had hired would make sure there were no "disagreeable occurrences." The school did operate successfully for a while, but lack of funds soon forced it to close. Few free black parents could pay even the "remarkably moderate" fees the school charged for their children's education, and whites were simply not prepared to let their slaves attend.

A School

Founded by an association of free people of color of the city of Washington, called the "Resolute Beneficial Society" . . . is now open for the reception of children of free people of color, and others that ladies and gentlemen may think proper to send, to be instructed in reading, writing, arithmetic, English grammar, or other branches of education, applicable to their capacities, by a steady, active and experienced teacher, whose attention is wholly devoted to the purposes described. It is presumed, that free colored families will embrace the advantages thus presented to them, either by subscribing to the funds of the society, or by sending their children to the school; the terms in either case being remarkably moderate. An improvement of the intellect and morals of colored youth being the leading object of this institution, the patronage of benevolent ladies and gentlemen, by donation or subscription, is humbly solicited in aid of the funds—the demands thereon being heavy, and the means at present much too limited . . . And, to avoid disagreeable occurrences, no writings are to be done by the teacher for a slave, neither directly nor indirectly to serve the purposes of a slave, on any account whatsoever. Further particulars may be known, by applying to any of the undersigned officers.

WILLIAM COSTIN, President
GEORGE HICKS, Vice President
JAMES HARRIS, Secretary
GEORGE BELL, Treasurer
ARCHIBALD JOHNSON, Marshal
FRED LEWIS, Chairman of the Committee
ISAAC JOHNSON, Committee
SCIPIO BEENS, Committee

Source: *Daily National Intelligencer* (Washington, D.C.), August 29, 1818

∼

South Carolina's Black Code (1822)

Denmark Vesey's 1822 plot to seize control of the city of Charleston and liberate the slaves shook whites in South Carolina to the core. The fact that Vesey was a

*free man, not a slave, and that he was a successful craftsman with his own home
and business was something they found especially unnerving. What they failed to
understand was that Vesey had been a slave until he won the money in a lottery to
buy his freedom. He also had close ties to the slave community. He had numerous
family members who were still enslaved. The authorities executed Vesey and his
co-conspirators, all of whom were slaves, and then they passed a sweeping new
law in an effort to keep the free black community under tight control and prevent
any more rebellions. "An Act for the better regulation of free negroes and persons
of colour" was one of the harshest black codes in force anywhere in the nation. It
stipulated, among other things, that*

[N]o free negro or person of colour, who shall leave this state, shall be suffered to return . . .

[E]very free male negro or person of colour, between the age of fifteen and
fifty years, within this state, who may not be a native of said state . . . shall
pay a tax of fifty dollars per annum . . .

[I]f any vessel shall come into any port or harbor of this state, from any
other state or foreign port, having on board any free negroes or persons of
colour as cooks, stewards, mariners, or in any other employment on board
of said vessel, such free negroes or persons of colour shall be liable to be
seized and confined in jail, until said vessel shall clear out and depart from
this state . . . And . . . the captain of said vessel shall be bound to carry
away the said free negro or free person of colour, and to pay the expenses
of his detention, and in case of his neglect or refusal so to do . . . such free
negroes or persons of colour shall be deemed and taken as absolute slaves,
and sold. . . .

[E]very free male negro, mulatto or mestizo in this state, above the age of
fifteen years, shall be compelled to have a guardian, who shall be a respectable freeholder of the district in which said free negro, mulatto or mestizo
shall reside; and it shall be the duty of the said guardian to go before the clerk
of the court of the said district . . . and . . . give to the clerk his certificate,
that the said negro, mulatto or mestizo . . . is of good character and correct
habits . . .

[I]f any person or persons shall counsel, aid, or hire any slave or slaves, free
negroes, or persons of colour, to raise a rebellion . . . such person or persons
on conviction thereof, shall be adjudged felons, and suffer death.

Source: *Charleston City Gazette*, January 6, 1823

∽

Emigration to Haiti (1824–1825)

In 1817, black Philadelphians had roundly rejected the idea of leaving America for West Africa. Black people elsewhere were equally hostile. However, when the president of Haiti announced his resettlement plan, he found many eager recruits. To thousands of free blacks the idea of emigrating to an independent black republic in the Americas was much more appealing than venturing off to a white-run colony in Africa. "Doctor" Belfast Burton (ca. 1775–1849), a skilled healer from Philadelphia, leaped at the chance to go to Haiti. Most of the emigrants soon returned to the United States disappointed and disillusioned, but Burton was full of enthusiasm, as his letter to his old friend Richard Allen shows. (It is worth noting, though, that Burton himself eventually came back to live in Philadelphia.)

I will remark that no man can have any just conception of the country without seeing it, and I had no idea of there being any such place on the globe . . . It is well known there are some people who will not be satisfied in any place nor any situation, but those here generally express the highest satisfaction, and say it surpasses their most sanguine expectations. . . . [T]he government gives them the land as promised, and all, whether mechanics, or of any other occupation, receive the like quantity; and if any choose to rent, they still receive their land . . . they receive their four months provisions, and if that does not prove sufficient, they have assurances from [the] government, to be supported, until they can support themselves. The preparations for schools are making. Their religious freedom is most perfect . . . As to war, by invasion from the French, we have scarcely heard anything about it . . . I could say much more, but time will not admit . . .

BELFAST BURTON

Source: *Spectator* (New York), February 25, 1825

～

The Birth of the Black Press (1827)

In 1827, a group of black community leaders in New York City began publishing Freedom's Journal. *Their immediate goal was to refute racist attacks upon them in the mainstream press, but their longer-term goal was to ensure that black people had their own newspaper that would reflect their needs and concerns. The man they chose as the paper's editor was John Brown Russwurm, one of the first black men to receive a college degree.* Freedom's Journal *enjoyed an extensive circulation and had agents throughout the North and in the West Indies. The following address "To*

Our Patrons" appeared on page 1 of the first edition of the paper and speaks to the bold agenda of its founders. Freedom's Journal *survived for almost two years before Russwurm's defection to the American Colonization Society, coupled with financial problems, forced its editorial board to suspend publication.*

We wish to plead our own cause. Too long have others spoken for us. Too long has the publick been deceived by misrepresentation, in things which concern us dearly . . . We are aware that there are many instances of vice among us, but we avow that it is because no one has taught its subjects to be virtuous; many instances of poverty, because no sufficient efforts accommodated to minds contracted by slavery, and deprived of early education have been made, to teach them how to husband their hard earnings, and to secure to themselves comforts.

Education being an object of the highest importance . . . we shall . . . urge upon our brethren the necessity and expediency of training their children, while young, in habits of industry, and thus forming them for becoming useful members of society . . .

The civil rights of a people being of the greatest value, it shall ever be our duty to vindicate our brethren, when oppressed, and to lay the case before the publick. We shall also urge upon our brethren, who are qualified by the laws of the different states, the expediency of using their elective franchise . . .

We trust also, that through the columns of the FREEDOM'S JOURNAL, many practical pieces, having for their bases, the improvement of our brethren, will be presented to them . . . Useful knowledge of every kind, and every thing that relates to Africa, shall find a ready admission into our columns; and as that vast continent becomes daily more known, we trust that many things will come to light, proving that the natives of it are neither so ignorant nor stupid as they have generally been supposed to be. And while these important subjects shall occupy the columns of the FREEDOM'S JOURNAL, we would not be unmindful of our brethren who are still in the iron fetters of bondage. They are our kindred by all the ties of nature; and though but little can be effected by us, let our sympathies be poured forth, and our prayers in their behalf, ascend to Him who is able to succour them . . .

In the spirit of candor and humility, we intend by a simple representation of facts to lay our case before the publick, with a view to arrest the progress of prejudice, and to shield ourselves against the consequent evils. We wish to conciliate all and to irritate none, yet we must be firm and unwavering in our principles, and persevering in our efforts . . .

In conclusion, whatever concerns us as a people, will ever find a ready admission into the FREEDOM'S JOURNAL . . . And while every thing in our power shall be performed to support the character of our Journal, we would respectfully invite our numerous friends to assist by their communications, and our coloured brethren to strengthen our hands by their subscriptions, as our labour is one of common cause, and worthy of their consideration and support.

THE EDITORS

Source: *Freedom's Journal*, March 16, 1827

⌢

David Walker on the Nature of Black Freedom (1829)

Originally from Wilmington, North Carolina, David Walker (ca. 1796–1830) was free because his mother was free, although his father was probably a slave. As a young man, Walker lived for a time in Charleston, South Carolina before moving to Boston around 1825, where he married, opened a used-clothing store, and soon established himself as a member of the city's activist black elite. Among other things, he was the local agent for the pioneering black newspaper Freedom's Journal, *and a founding member of the Massachusetts General Colored Association. He is best remembered as the author of* An Appeal to the Coloured Citizens of the World *(1829). The* Appeal, *with its forthright condemnation of slavery and racism, enraged white Southerners. Walker used his contacts in the seafaring community to smuggle copies of his pamphlet into the South, where he hoped they would get into the hands of both the slaves and the free blacks. When Walker died from tuberculosis the year after the* Appeal *was published, rumors swirled that he had in fact been murdered for daring to speak out.*

Men of colour, who are also of sense, for you particularly is my APPEAL designed. Our more ignorant brethren are not able to penetrate its value. I call upon you therefore to cast your eyes upon the wretchedness of your brethren, and to do your utmost to enlighten them . . . Do any of you say that you and your family are free and happy, and what have you to do with the wretched slaves and other people? So can I say, for I enjoy as much freedom as any of you, if I am not quite as well off as the best of you. Look into our freedom and happiness, and see of what kind they are composed! They are of the very lowest kind—they are the very *dregs!*—they are the most servile and abject kind, that ever a people was in possession of! If any of you wish to know how FREE you are, let one of you start and go through the southern and western States of this country, and unless you travel as a slave to a white man (a servant is a *slave* to the man he serves) or have your free papers, (which if you are not careful they will get from you) if they do not take you up and put you in jail, and if you cannot give good evidence of your freedom, sell you into eternal slavery, I am not a living man . . . And yet some of you have the hardihood to say that you are free and happy! May God have mercy on your freedom and happiness!!

Source: Peter P. Hinks, ed., *David Walker's "Appeal to the Coloured Citizens of the World"* (University Park: Pennsylvania State University Press, 2000), 30–31.

~

An African-American Shipowner Visits Charleston (ca. 1830)

One of the people white abolitionist Samuel J. May met on a visit to New Bedford, Massachusetts, was black merchant and shipowner Richard Johnson (1776–1853). In a long career at sea, Johnson had risen "from cabin boy to captain." When the episode he recounted to May took place, he was sailing on one of his own vessels. He and the white captain did not anticipate any trouble when they put into Charleston for a few days, but almost immediately Johnson found himself facing arrest. South Carolina's infamous Negro Seamen's Act required that all black crew members entering the port be jailed until their ship departed. However, the law assumed that the only black men on board a vessel would be sailors, cooks, or stewards. The authorities did not know how to deal with a black man who actually owned the vessel.

Mr. Johnson, a few years ago, freighted a small vessel for the West Indies, and went with her as supercargo. On his return, he found occasion to put into the port of Charleston, S.C. The cook of the vessel, and one of the sailors, being colored, were immediately thrown into prison. And the "officers of Justice" were proceeding to deal likewise with Mr. Johnson, when several gentlemen who were acquainted with him . . . interfered. They insisted, that according to the language of the law, the magistrates had no authority to commit Mr. Johnson, he being neither cook, sailor, nor stevedore. The Mayor demurred some time, because as he said, such a man might do more harm among the slaves, than if he had not risen from the menial situation, to which the free blacks are normally condemned. Nevertheless, as Mr. J. and his counselors appealed to the law, and also gave bonds for his good behavior, the honorable Mayor was obliged to leave him at liberty; but admonished him that if he ever came to Charleston again, he should not be protected by the letter of the law.

Source: *Liberator* (Boston), April 24, 1835

~

Maria W. Stewart's Speeches (1832–1833)

Born in Hartford, Connecticut, Maria Miller (1803–1879) was orphaned at age five and bound out as a servant. After her term of indenture ended, she continued working as a domestic. Eventually she moved to Boston, and in 1826 she married James W. Stewart, a much older black businessman. As the wife of one of Boston's wealthiest men of color, Maria Miller Stewart enjoyed a comfortable existence, but in 1829 her husband died and his white executors cheated her out of her inheritance. The following year she lost her friend and mentor, David Walker. Deeply spiritual, with a tremendous love of learning and a growing commitment to abolition and social reform, Stewart began writing and lecturing. Her willingness to defy the conventions of gender as well as race, to speak to "promiscuous" audiences (i.e., men as well as women) and to criticize black men for what she regarded as their failings aroused opposition within the black community. In 1833, Stewart left Boston for New York City, where she became a teacher. As the first excerpt shows, Stewart believed young black women should have better access to education and more job opportunities. The second excerpt is from a speech Stewart gave at Boston's African Masonic Hall that no doubt irked many of the men in attendance.

I have asked several individuals of my own sex, who transact business for themselves, if, providing our girls were to give them the most satisfactory references, they would not be willing to grant them an equal opportunity with others? Their reply has been—for their own part, they had no objection; but as it was not the custom, were they to take them into their employ, they would be in danger of losing the public patronage. And such is the powerful force of prejudice—Let our girls possess what amiable qualities of soul they may—let their characters be fair and spotless as innocence itself—let their natural taste and ingenuity be what they may—it is impossible for scarce an individual of them to rise above the condition of servants. . . . As servants, we are respected; but let us presume to aspire any higher [and] our employer regards us no longer. I do not consider it derogatory, my friends, for persons to live out to service . . . and I would highly commend the performance of almost any thing for an honest livelihood . . . [but most] of our color have dragged out a miserable existence of servitude from the cradle to the grave . . . O, ye fairer sisters, whose hands are never soiled . . . Had we the opportunity that you have had, to improve our moral and mental faculties, what would have hindered our intellects from being as bright, and our manners from being as dignified as yours?

Source: *Liberator* (Boston), November 17, 1832

I would ask, is it blindness of mind, or stupidity of soul, or the want of education, that has caused our men who are 60 or 70 years of age never to let their voices be heard nor their hands be raised in behalf of their color? Or has it been for the fear of offending the whites? If it has, O ye fearful ones, throw off your fearfulness and come forth in the name of the Lord . . . If you are men, convince them that you possess the spirit of men . . . Have the sons of Africa no souls? Shall the chains of ignorance forever confine them? Shall the insipid appellation of "clever negroes" or "good creatures" any longer content them? . . . It is true, our fathers bled and died in the revolutionary war, and others fought bravely under the command of Jackson, in defence [sic] of liberty. But where is the man that has distinguished himself in these modern days by acting wholly in the defence of African rights and liberty? . . . Talk, without effort, is nothing; you are abundantly capable, gentlemen, of making yourselves men of distinction; and this gross neglect, on your part, causes my blood to boil within me . . . Cast your eyes about—look as far as you can see—all, all is owned by the lordly white, except here and there a lowly dwelling which the man of color, midst deprivations, fraud and opposition, has been scarce able to procure . . . We have pursued the shadow, they [whites] have obtained the substance; we have performed the labor, they have received the profits.

Source: *Liberator* (Boston), April 27, 1833

～

Free Blacks in Business in Antebellum America

John Remond, a Salem, Massachusetts caterer, used the sighting of a sea serpent off the New England coast to appeal to potential customers. Philadelphia's Serena Gardiner emphasized her respectability and that of her establishment. While Gardiner offered accommodation to genteel African Americans, in South Carolina tailor turned hotelier Jehu Jones boasted of the splendors of his establishment to white planters and their families eager to escape the summer heat. In Boston, William and Thomas Jinnings understood the need to be as versatile as possible when it came to the inventory in their store and the skills they mastered. Black people in communities large and small looked for economic opportunities wherever they could find them and appreciated the importance of a good newspaper advertisement.

Nothing Like The Serpent

The public are hereby informed, that a more palatable fish than a Sea-Serpent will make his appearance on Monday next, at the new establishment in Front Street, and will not come alone, but in such quantities as may best suit purchasers. The supposition is that few of my customers can swallow a *serpent*, and but few that are not fond of swallowing an OYSTER. *Now know ye,*

Gentlemen of Salem and vicinity, that an OYSTER ESTABLISHMENT will be opened on Monday next . . . where the best of Oysters and good attendance will be provided.

> Let them be roasted, stew'd or fried,
> Or any other way beside,
> You'll well be serv'd, or ill betide
> JOHN REMOND

Source: *Salem Gazette*, September 2, 1817

Sullivan's Island Establishment

For the accommodation of visitors the Proprietor has purchased a Carriage and a pair of very gentle Horses, to take Ladies and Gentlemen up to the east end of the Island; and a Horse and Gig, also for the use of his friends.

Having spared no expense to make the Establishment as comfortable as possible, and to make the charges as low as the very high expense of the Establishment will admit, [he] has placed the different charges as follows:

For Boarding, per week, for one person $14.00
For Dinner for one person 1.25
For Supper ditto 0.50
For Bed ditto 0.50
For Breakfast ditto.. 0.50
Children half price
Servants ditto
  ICE CREAM every day

JEHU JONES

Source: *City Gazette and Daily Advertiser* (Charleston, South Carolina), July 19, 1817

Genteel Private Boarding House

MRS. SERENA GARDINER, who formerly kept a private boarding-house at No. 19, Powell-street, has removed to No. 13, ELIZABETH-STREET; where respectable persons of color can be accommodated with Boarding, and also with separate apartments if required. A share of patronage is respectfully solicited.

Source: *Liberator* (Boston), May 9, 1835

REMOVAL—W. S. & T. JINNINGS respectfully announce to their friends and the public that they have removed to the spacious store, No. 100 Court Street, adjoining Blaney's Grate Factory, where they now carry on the regular business of a clothing and variety store on an entirely new plan.

Their stock will consist of every variety of curious and fancy articles—also Watches and Jewelry, Guns, Swords, Pistols, &c. Surgical, Mathematical, Nautical and Musical Instruments, Carpenter's tools—also a large number of rare and interesting Prints, an assortment of military equipment, such as Caps, Belts, Silk Sashes, Coats, &c., together with a first rate assortment of new and second [hand] fashionable Clothing, Stocks, Collars, Bosoms, Suspenders, Handkerchiefs, Gloves and Hosiery, constantly on hand at low prices.

Source: *Liberator* (Boston), May 12, 1837

Thomas Jinnings, Practical Surgeon Dentist

All dental operations, from cleansing teeth to inserting them on gold plate, skillfully executed. Teeth plugged in a manner superior to any plan ever before practiced in this country, by which the original shape of the tooth can be perfectly restored. All operations warranted. At Dr. Mann's office, No. 16 Summer Street, Boston.

Source: *Colored American* (New York), August 22, 1840

～

On the Impact of Prejudice (1837)

In 1837, in an effort to understand the impact of racial prejudice in the North, white abolitionist Angelina Grimké contacted several well-educated and articulate African-American women whom she knew through various antislavery organizations and asked them to share with her what prejudice meant in their everyday lives. Sarah Louisa Forten, one of the daughters of wealthy Philadelphia businessman James Forten, responded, describing her own experiences and her awareness that even among white abolitionists there were subtle undercurrents of racism. Forten was an accomplished writer. Using the pen-name "Ada," she composed poetry for antislavery newspapers like William Lloyd Garrison's Liberator. She was a founding member of the interracial Philadelphia Female Anti-Slavery Society and she had a deep admiration for many of the white people she encountered through her antislavery work. Even so, she realized that a commitment to ending slavery did not always translate into a rejection of racial prejudice.

In reply to your question—of the "effect of Prejudice" on myself, I must acknowledge that it has often embittered my feelings, particularly when I recollect that we are the innocent victims of it—for you are well aware that it originates from dislike to the color of the skin, as much as from the degradation of Slavery—I am peculiarly sensitive on this point, and consequently seek to avoid as much as possible . . . mingling with those who exist under its influence. I must own that it has often engendered feelings of discontent and mortification in my breast when I saw that many were preferred before me, who by education—birth—or worldly circumstances were no better than myself—*their* sole claim to notice depending on the superior advantage of being *white*—but I am striving to live above such heart burnings—and will learn to "bear and forbear" believing that a spirit of forbearance under such evils is all that we as a people can well exert . . .

Even our professed friends have not yet rid themselves of it [prejudice]—to some of them it clings like a dark mantle obscuring their many virtues and choking up the avenues to higher and nobler sentiments. I recollect the words of one of the best and least prejudiced men in the Abolition ranks. Ah said he—"I can recall the time when in walking with a Colored brother, the darker the night, the better Abolitionist was I."

Source: Sarah L. Forten to Angelina Grimké, April 15, 1837, in Gilbert H. Barnes and Dwight L. Dumond, eds., *Letters of Theodore Dwight Weld, Angelina Grimké Weld, and Sarah Grimké, 1822–1844* (New York: D. Appleton-Century, 1934), vol. 1, pp. 379–81.

∼

Kidnappers (1840–1841)

Long before the passage of the infamous Fugitive Slave Act of 1850, free blacks knew that whether they lived in the North or the South they had to be on their guard. Empowered by the 1793 federal Fugitive Slave Law, slave owners and their agents roamed communities in every part of the nation hunting for escaped slaves. Professional slave catchers who had only a vague description of the missing slaves could and did make mistakes and claim as fugitives people who were legally free. And sometimes this was anything but a genuine case of mistaken identity on the part of an overzealous slave catcher or a slave owner who did not recall exactly what his slaves looked like. The following two reports speak for themselves. Flora Way was quick-witted and faced down the two men who accosted her in the street. Fred Roberts presumably acted upon the tip from the North Carolina informant and hastily left town.

Look Out for Kidnappers—I

Mrs. Flora Way, who resides in Mercer street, in this city [New York], and is a member of the Abyssinian Baptist Church in Anthony street, while walking [along] Broadway on Friday, the 27th ultimo, between White and Walker streets, was accosted by two individuals supposed to be from Georgia, as they thought Mrs. Way was a fugitive slave from that State. Mrs. Way is from Savannah, and knows all about that horrible system which is grinding the souls and bodies of two and a half million of her brethren into the dust; and she gave them to know that she knew of no master but Christ, and that they had better refrain from molesting her.

Source: *Colored American* (New York), April 4, 1840

Look Out For Kidnappers—II

We have had handed to us a note, post marked Wilmington, N.C., and giving the information that a man by the name of Ricks, somewhere in the interior of this State [New York], has a plan on foot to betray one Fred Roberts, now said to be at work in Buffalo, into the hands of someone who would call himself master, and warning Fred to be upon his guard. We do not know how much truth there may be in this affair, though the letter lays before us, nor how many Ricks there may be in the State, and if many, which of them it may be; but one thing we know, that it is safe to forewarn Fred . . . and advise him that he is safe only in Canada. He may, before he is aware of it, find himself in the hands of a Buffalo constable, and locked up in [a] Buffalo jail.

Source: *Colored American* (New York), May 1, 1841

⁓

Class Differences among Antebellum Black Philadelphians (1841)

Joseph Willson (1817–1895) was born in Augusta, Georgia, one of five children of a wealthy Irish banker, John Willson, and Betsy Keating, a former slave. Before he died in 1822, John Willson wrote a will providing for his family and naming a trusted friend to be their guardian, since in Georgia free people of color were not considered legally competent to manage their own affairs. In the early 1830s, Betsy and her guardian decided that the family must move to the North to escape Georgia's increasing harsh restrictions on free blacks. They relocated to Philadelphia, where Joseph Willson trained as a printer before becoming a dentist. Well-read and articulate, he hoped that in his Sketches of the Higher Classes of Colored Society in Philadelphia *he could enlighten whites about class differences within the African-American community. He was frankly irritated at the tendency of whites to lump all free black people together as poor, lazy, and criminally-inclined.*

The public—or at least the great body, who have not been at the pains to make an examination—have long been accustomed to regard the people of color as one consolidated mass, all huddled together, without any particular or general distinctions, social or otherwise. The sight of one colored man with them, whatever may be his apparent condition, (provided it is any thing but genteel!) is the sight of a community; and the errors and crimes of one, [are] adjudged as the criterion of character of the whole body . . .

Taking the whole body of the colored population in the city of Philadelphia, they present in a gradual, moderate, and limited ratio, almost every grade of character, wealth, and . . . education. They are to be seen in ease, comfort and the enjoyment of all the social blessings of this life, and . . . they are to be found in the lowest depths of human degradation, misery, and want. They are also presented in the intermediate stages—sober, honest, industrious and respectable—claiming neither 'poverty nor riches,' yet maintaining . . . their families in comparative ease and comfort.

Source: Julie Winch, ed., *The Elite of Our People: Joseph Willson's Sketches of Black Upper-Class Life in Antebellum Philadelphia* (University Park: Pennsylvania State University Press, 2000), 82–83.

⌣

The Antislavery Cause and Guilt by Association (1843)

Joseph Stanly was a member of a prominent free black slaveholding family in New Bern, North Carolina. His father, John Carruthers Stanly, had been born a slave, but as a free man he had no qualms about buying slaves and putting them to work in his barbershop and on the plantations he owned. The elder Stanly's support of the slave system earned him a measure of respect from influential whites in his neighborhood. However, as a young man, Benjamin Stanly, one of John

C. *Stanly's sons, and Joseph's twin, rejected slavery. He moved to Philadelphia, went into business as a barber, and became a staunch supporter of abolition. The repercussions for Joseph when he returned home to North Carolina after visiting Benjamin in Philadelphia were nothing short of disastrous, as the following letter explained.*

Joseph Stanly, (a colored young man of New Bern, North Carolina) a few months ago, came on to this city [Philadelphia] to see a twin brother . . . whom he had not seen for several years. Previous to leaving, he was assured by those "high in authority," "that there would not be the least difficulty in returning home; that he might stay in Philadelphia just as long as he saw fit, and return and remain here unmolested." In fact, many said, "Why, Joseph, why need you have any fears of being disturbed: you certainly know your standing in the community, and what a favorable character your father has borne amongst us for the last forty or fifty years; and do you suppose we could be so unkind as to prevent his son from returning home to those whom we have always respected!" Being thus assured, he left his home . . . arrived in Philadelphia, and spent several months with his brother; after which, he returned back to the land of his birth . . . But scarcely had his feet retouched that soil . . . than he received, from the hands of an officer, the very friendly and humane notice, '*that he must leave the town within 24 hours, never to enter it again.*' 'Was I not assured, previous to my departure, that I should return and remain here unmolested?' 'Yes, sir.' 'Well, what does this mean?' 'Why, it means this, that we don't intend to have an abolitionist in *this 'ere town.*' 'But, sir, what evidence have you that I am an abolitionist?' Whether you are or not, YOUR BROTHER IS, and it is reported that HE spoke at an abolition meeting . . . That is sufficient, and you must leave.'

Source: *Liberator* (Boston), January 6, 1843

～

A Black Southerner's Experiences in New York (ca. 1845)

James Thomas was born in Nashville, Tennessee, in 1827. His mother, Sally Thomas, was a slave, and his father, John Catron, was a white lawyer. Catron did nothing for his son, but Sally Thomas ran her own laundry and earned the money to buy James's freedom. In the mid-1840s, Thomas, by then a successful barber, agreed to close his shop for a while and travel to the North as a servant to a wealthy white Southerner. Thomas was unimpressed with the treatment he received in the "free" North. (Ironically, Thomas's father became an associate justice of the U.S. Supreme Court and concurred with the majority in the Dred Scott case that blacks "had no rights which the white man was bound to respect.")

I soon learned something about New York that did not please me. I remarked that I wanted to go to the museum. I was told not to go, that I wouldn't be admitted unless I was with my boss or had one of his children . . . I said I would like to ride up town in an Omnibus. I was told they wouldn't carry me unless I was with a white person or child. I learned afterwards that if a colored face got inside of an Omnibus, the white passengers would leap out as though a case of small pox or a ghost had entered . . .

It seemed very strange to those colored people from the south who went north the first time. They were grinned and hooted at. Some hoodlum would holler "black cloud rising." Often thrown at, or jumped on and roughly handled, unless the col[ore]d [man] ran for his life. No where south such things ever occurred, that I saw, which was easy enough to understand. In clubbing or abusing the Negro they would find they had abused a piece of property that had a protector.

Source: Loren Schweninger, ed., *From Tennessee Slave to St. Louis Entrepreneur: The Autobiography of James Thomas* (Columbia: University of Missouri Press, 1984), 123–24.

～

Tribute to a Civic Leader in California (1848)

A successful merchant, shipowner, land speculator, and diplomat, William Alexander Leidesdorff (1810–1848) was one of the leading citizens of San Francisco in the 1840s. Although he was a naturalized Mexican citizen, Leidesdorff supported the movement to break California away from Mexico and annex it to the United States. This account of Leidesdorff's short but remarkable life, reprinted in New York from a California newspaper, identifies him as being "of Danish parentage." That is accurate—to a point. While his father was Danish, his mother was a woman of color. Had Leidesdorff lived longer, he might well have emerged as a major power broker in California politics. He died without heirs, and claimants fought for decades over his vast fortune.

Died, at his own residence, in this place, at 1 o'clock, a.m. on the 18th inst. after an illness of seven days . . . WILLIAM A. LEIDESDORFF, Esq., late U.S. Vice

Consul for this port. Having received the consolations of the Catholic religion during his illness, he was buried yesterday . . . in the Mission Church of Dolores, near San Francisco. One of the largest and most respectable assemblages ever witnessed in this place followed the deceased from his late residence to the place of interment, and every thing was done on the part of the community to evince its deep feeling for the loss it has sustained. All places of business and public entertainment were closed—the flags of the garrison and the shipping were flying at half mast, and minute guns were discharged from the barracks and the shipping as the procession moved from town . . .

Captain Leidesdorff was of Danish parentage, but was a native of the West Indies . . . He was formerly well known as a merchant captain in the ports of New Orleans and New York but for the last seven years he has been in business on this coast, where he has gained a high character for integrity, enterprise and activity. In private life he was social[,] liberal and hospitable to an eminent degree . . . As a merchant and a citizen, he was generous, enterprising and public spirited and his name is intimately identified with the growth and prosperity of San Francisco. It is no injustice . . . to say that the town has lost its most valuable resident . . . His energy of character and business enterprises have so blended his history with that of San Francisco that all classes deplore his death as a great public calamity. While many mourn for his various social virtues, in Capt. Leidesdorff the laboring classes of the community and the poor have lost a munificent patron and a generous friend.

Source: *New York Herald*, September 27, 1848

～

Martin R. Delany on African-American Emigration (1852)

Born in Virginia, the son of a free woman and a slave, Martin Robison Delany (1812–1885) moved to Pittsburgh, Pennsylvania, when he was in his teens and embarked on a remarkable career as a physician, a newspaper editor, and a champion for civil rights. He was very forthright in his 1852 book The Condition, Elevation, Emigration, and Destiny of the Colored People of the United States. *It was time for the free black community to reconsider the whole question of emigration, he insisted. As Delany saw it, African Americans had no alternative but to leave the United States because whites had no intention of treating them as equals. While he was not sure where they should go, he believed they must go. "We are a nation within a nation," he declared. "We must go from our oppressors." Freedom for black people was a sham, Delany maintained, and they needed to realize that.*

[T]he bondman is disfranchised, and for the most part so are we. He is denied all civil, religious, and social privileges . . . and so are we. They [the slaves] have no part . . . in the government of the country, neither have we. They are ruled and governed without representation, existing as mere nonentities among the citizens, and excrescences on the body politic . . . and so are we. Where then is our political superiority to the enslaved? None, neither are we superior in any other relation to society, except that we are de facto masters of ourselves and joint rulers of our own domestic household, while the bondman's self is claimed by another, and his relation to his family denied him . . .

In . . . the United States, there are *three million, five hundred thousand slaves*; and we, the nominally free, are *six hundred thousand* in number; estimating one-sixth to be men, we have *one hundred thousand* able-bodied freemen, which will make a powerful auxiliary in any country to which we may become adopted—an ally not to be despised by any power on earth. We love our country, dearly love her, but she don't love us—she despises us, and bids us begone, driving us from her embraces; but we shall not go where she desires us; but when we do go, whatever love we have for her, we shall love the country none the less that receives us as her adopted children.

Source: Martin R. Delany, *The Condition, Elevation, Emigration and Destiny of the Colored People of the United States* (Philadelphia: The Author, 1852; reprint Baltimore: Black Classic Press, 1993), 14–15, 203.

～

Segregation on Public Transportation (1854)

Generations before Rosa Parks refused to move to the back of the bus in Montgomery, Alabama, African Americans in many communities were protesting the discriminatory treatment they routinely received on trains, steamboats, and omnibuses. They paid their fare and were refused passage. They purchased first-class tickets and were sent to the vastly inferior "colored car." Elizabeth Jennings, a well-connected and genteel teacher in New York City, was on her way to church one Sunday when she and a friend tried to ride the street car. After being forcibly ejected from the all-white car, Jennings successfully sued the street car company. This is her account of the episode that led up to the lawsuit.

Sarah E. Adams and myself walked down to the corner of Pearl and Chatham Sts. to take the Third Ave. cars. We got on the platform when the conductor told us to wait for the next car. I told him I could not wait, as I was in a hurry to go to church.

He then told me that the other car had my people in it, that it was appro-priated for "my people." I told him . . . I wished to go to church and I did not wish to be detained . . . I told him I was a respectable person, born and raised in New York, did not know where he was born, and that he was a good-for-nothing impudent fellow for insulting decent persons while on their way to church. He then said he would put me out. I told him not to lay hands on me. He took hold of me and I took hold of the window sash. He pulled me until he broke my grasp . . . He then ordered the driver to . . . come and help him . . . Both seized hold of me by the arms and pulled and dragged me down on the bottom of the platform.

Source: *Frederick Douglass' Paper*, July 28, 1854

～

Black Life in Charleston (1857)

George E. Stephens (1832–1888), a Northern-born craftsman, was unprepared for what he experienced when he spent a few days in Charleston, South Carolina in 1857. In accordance with South Carolina's Negro Seamen's Act, he was arrested and jailed when the ship he was serving on arrived in port. The captain interceded with the authorities and Stephens was eventually set free. Once he was released, he had the chance to "see the sights," as he recounted in a letter to a friend back home. What he saw and heard disgusted him. Ironically, during the Civil War Stephens returned to Charleston, this time as a soldier in a black Union regiment.

A few days after my perambulation about the streets of Charleston I met a young man . . . with whom I had become acquainted in Phil[adelphia]. I wished him to take a cigar with me . . . He informed me that it was against the law for a Colored man to smoke a cigar or walk with a cane in the streets of Charleston. And if the streets (sidewalk) are crowded the negro must take the middle of the street. I met several white men, they did not pretend to move an inch—so I had always to give way to them. I have been informed since if I had run against one of them, they would have had me flogged. Poor wretches. Little do they accomplish by such trivial proscriptions. [S]uch miserable oppression serves not one single degree to curb the spirit of even a crushed and injured African.

Source: George E. Stephens to Jacob C. White Jr., 8 January 1858, in C. Peter Ripley et al., eds., *The Black Abolitionist Papers* (Chapel Hill: University of North Carolina Press, 1991), vol. 4, pp. 371–73.

～

John S. Rock on the Likelihood of War (1858)

New Jersey native John Swett Rock (1825–1866) was truly a "renaissance man." A physician and a teacher, he also trained as a lawyer. In 1861, he qualified as a member of the Massachusetts Bar—he had moved to Boston in 1852—and in 1865 he was admitted to practice before the U.S. Supreme Court. He was an outspoken advocate of racial equality, a fierce opponent of slavery, and a champion of rights for women as well as men. The following excerpt is from a speech Rock gave in Boston on March 5, 1858, in commemoration of the Boston Massacre. He was certain that there would soon be a war against slavery and that African Americans would determine the outcome of that conflict.

White Americans have taken great pains to try to prove that we are cowards . . . The black man is not a coward . . . Nothing but a superior force keeps us down. And when I see the slaves rising up by hundreds annually, in the majesty of human nature, bidding defiance to every slave code and its penalties, making the issue Canada or death, I am disposed to ask if the charge of cowardice does not come with an ill-grace . . . Our fathers fought nobly for freedom, but they were not victorious. They fought for liberty, but they got slavery. The white man benefitted, but the black man was injured. I do not envy the white American the little liberty which he enjoys . . . But I would have all men free . . . Sooner or later, the clashing of arms will be heard in this country, and the black man's services will be needed: 150,000 freemen capable of bearing arms, and not all cowards and fools, and three quarter of a million slaves, wild with the enthusiasm caused by the dawn of the glorious opportunity of being able to strike a genuine blow for freedom, will be a power which white men will be "bound to respect." Will the blacks fight? Of course they will. The black man will never be neutral . . . White men may despise, ridicule, slander and abuse us, and make us feel degraded; they may seek as they always have done to divide us and make us feel degraded; but no man shall cause me to turn my back upon my race.

Source: *Liberator* (Boston), March 12, 1858

～

Using Wealth to Buy Political Influence (1858)

St. Louis native Cyprian Clamorgan (1830–1902) was the grandson of a French adventurer, Jacques Clamorgan, and his black concubine, Susanne. Cyprian's early life was chaotic, and he remained illiterate until he was in his late teens, but once he learned to read and write there was no holding him back. In 1858, he authored a witty and perceptive analysis of the situation of free people of color in the city of his birth—a city where slavery flourished, but where there were several thousand free black people, some of them wealthy and well-connected. His message was clear enough: money equaled power, and affluent free blacks could make their voices heard. Even if they could not vote or run for office, they could influence their white tenants and people they did business with to support candidates who favored antislavery and equal rights.

[T]he colored people of St. Louis command several millions of dollars; and everyone knows that money, in whose hands soever it may be found, has an influence proportioned to its amount. Now, although our colored friends have no voice in the elections, they are not idle spectators. They know what parties and what individuals are most favorable to their interests, and they are not slow in making friends with those who are able and willing to serve them. . . . [T]he wealthy free colored men of St. Louis . . . know that the abolition of slavery in Missouri would remove a stigma from their race, and elevate them in the scale of society. . . . When slavery is abolished, where will be found the power of excluding the colored man from an equal participation in the fruits of human progression and mutual development? What political party will then dare to erect a platform on which the black man cannot stand side by side with his white brother? . . . The colored men of St. Louis have no votes themselves, but they control a large number of votes at every election. Many of them own houses which are rented to white voters, and others trade extensively with white dealers. It is an easy matter to them to say to their white tenants . . . "[V]ote this ticket or seek another place of abode." It is no less easy for them to tell the merchant that, unless he votes for certain men, he will lose a large custom, and no one acquainted with human nature will deny that such requests are usually complied with.

Source: Julie Winch, ed., *Cyprian Clamorgan's "The Colored Aristocracy of St. Louis"* (Columbia: University of Missouri Press, 1999), pp. 47–48.

～

"Being a Citizen of the United States" (1859)

Even before the Dred Scott *decision declaring that blacks were not and never had been citizens, the U.S. State Department routinely refused to issue a passport to anyone whose paperwork indicated that they were black. Sarah Parker Remond (1826–1894), the daughter of Salem, Massachusetts, businessman John Remond, went to England in 1858 as an antislavery lecturer. Before she left the United States she applied for a passport. In an era before photographs, a written description sufficed—and Remond's simply stated that she was of a "dark complexion." Officials in Washington assumed she was white and she got her passport. Trouble ensued, however, when Remond went to the U.S. embassy in London to get a visa to travel to France.*

Sarah P. Remond to Hon. George M. Dallas, Dec. 12, 1859

Sir—I beg to inform you that a short time since I went to the office of the American embassy to have my passport visaed for France. I should remark that my passport is an American one, granted to me in the United States, and signed by the Minister in due form. It states—what is the fact—that I am a citizen of the United States. I was born in Massachusetts. Upon my asking to have my passport visaed at the American embassy, the person in the office refused to affix the visa on the ground that I am a person of color. Being a citizen of the United States, I respectfully demand as my right that my passport be visaed by the Minister of my country . . .

SARAH P. REMOND

Legation of the United States, London, Dec. 14, 1859
To Miss Sarah P. Remond

I am directed by the Minister to acknowledge the receipt of your note . . . and to say in reply, he must, of course, be sorry if any of his countrywomen, irrespective of color or extraction, should think him frivolously disposed to withhold from them facilities in his power to grant for travelling . . . but when the indispensable qualification for an American passport—that of the "United States citizenship"—does not exist, when, indeed, it is manifestly an impossibility by law that it should exist, a just sense of his official obligations . . . constrains him to say that the demand . . . cannot be complied with.

BENJ. MORAN, *Assistant Secretary of Legation*

Sarah P. Remond to Benjamin Moran

SIR—I have the honor to acknowledge the receipt of your letter . . . The purport of your communication is most extraordinary. You now lay down the rule that persons free born in the United States, and who have been subjected all their lives to the taxation and other burdens imposed upon American citizens, are to be deprived of their rights as such, merely because their complexion happens to be dark, and that they are to be refused the aid of the Ministers of their country, whose salaries they contribute to pay.

Source: *New York Herald*, January 24, 1860

Notes

Chapter One

1. Louisiana *Code Noir* (1724), article 54, in B. F. Finch, ed., *Historical Collections of Louisiana: Embracing Translations of Many Rare and Valuable Documents* (New York: D. Appleton, 1851), vol. 3, p. 95.

2. William Waller Hening, comp., *Statutes at Large, Being a Collection of all the Laws of Virginia from the First Session of the Legislature in the Year 1619* (Richmond: R. & W. & G. Bartow, 1819–1823), vol. 2, p. 267.

3. "An Act Concerning Negroes & Other Slaves," in "Proceedings and Acts of the General Assembly, September 1664," *Archives of Maryland* (Baltimore: Maryland Historical Society, 1883), vol. 1, p. 533.

4. Hening, comp., *Statutes at Large of Virginia*, vol. 3, p. 86.

5. See, for example, *American Weekly Mercury* (Philadelphia), September 23–30, 1736.

6. *Pennsylvania Gazette*, March 5, 1751.

7. Massachusetts Body of Liberties (1641), www.winthropsociety.com/liberties.php (accessed March 15, 2013)

8. *Boston News-Letter*, August 18, 1768.

Chapter Two

1. Summation of John Adams in *Rex v. Wemms*, in *Legal Papers of John Adams*, vol. 3, case 64, Massachusetts Historical Society, Adams Papers, Digital Edition (www.masshist.org, accessed September 6, 2013).

2. "Crispus Attucks" (1888), in James Jeffrey Roche, ed., *The Life of John Boyle O'Reilly, Together with His Complete Poems and Speeches* (New York: Cassell, 1891), 410.

3. Broadside, "Circular letter signed in behalf of our fellow slaves in this province, and by order of this committee, by Peter Bestes and others" [Boston, 1773], in Early American Imprints, series 1, no. 42416.

4. Constitution of Vermont, 1777, chapter 1, article 1, http://Vermontarchives. org/govhistory/constitute/con77.htm (accessed September 6, 2013)

5. "Minutes from the Case of *Commonwealth v. Nathaniel Jennison*," www. lexisnexis.com/academic/1univ/hist/aa/aas_case.asp (accessed September 6, 2013). Jennison claimed ownership of Walker.

6. *New Hampshire Gazette*, July 15, 1779.

7. New Hampshire Constitution (1783), articles 1 and 2, www.nh.gov/ constitution/constitution.html (accessed September 6, 2013).

8. The Act was reprinted in a number of Massachusetts newspapers. See, for instance, *Hampshire Chronicle* (Springfield), April 30, 1788.

9. The letters exchanged between the Newport and Philadelphia societies are reprinted in William Douglass, *Annals of the First African Church in the United States of America, Now Styled the African Episcopal Church of St. Thomas* (Philadelphia: King and Baird, 1862), 25–29.

Chapter Three

1. *Federal Gazette*, July 16, 1810.

2. *Copy of a Letter from Benjamin Banneker to the Secretary of State with his Answer* (Philadelphia: Daniel Lawrence, 1792), 8.

Chapter Four

1. Julie Winch, ed., *"The Elite of Our People": Joseph Willson's Sketches of Black Upper-Class Life in Antebellum Philadelphia* (University Park: Pennsylvania State University Press, 2000), 82–83.

2. Peter P. Hinks, ed., *David Walker's "Appeal to the Coloured Citizens of the World"* (University Park: Pennsylvania State University Press, 2000), 31.

3. John B. Russwurm to R. R. Gurley, May 7, 1829, ACS Correspondence, Incoming (American Colonization Society Papers, Library of Congress).

4. *Liberator*, March 2, 1833.

5. Sarah L. Forten to Angelina Grimké, April 15, 1837, in Gilbert H. Barnes and Dwight L. Dumond, eds., *Letters of Theodore Dwight Weld, Angelina Grimké Weld, and Sarah Grimké, 1822–1844* (New York: D. Appleton-Century, 1934), vol. 1, p. 381.

6. For the text of David Wilmot's speech see http://herb.ashp.cuny.edu/items/ show/1247 (accessed July 12, 2013).

Chapter Five

1. Editorial in *Frederick Douglass' Paper*, August 20, 1852.

2. Quoted in Ira Berlin, *Slaves Without Masters: The Free Negro in the Antebellum South* (New York: Pantheon, 1974), 164.

3. Martin R. Delany, *The Condition, Elevation, Emigration and Destiny of the Colored People of the United States* (Philadelphia: The Author, 1852; reprint Baltimore: Black Classic Press, 1993), 203.

4. "Fourth Debate with Stephen A. Douglas at Charleston, Illinois," in Roy P. Basler, ed., *The Collected Works of Abraham Lincoln* (New Brunswick, NJ: Rutgers University Press, 1953), vol. 3, pp. 145–46.

~

Suggested Readings

A generation ago, anyone hoping to learn very much about the lives of free black people in America from the colonial era to the Civil War faced a real challenge. By and large, this was uncharted territory. Fortunately, that is no longer the case. Over the past few decades scholars have mined a wide array of historical records to reveal the complexity of the "in between" world of those Americans who were not slaves but lacked the fundamental freedoms that whites considered to be their birthright.

Leon F. Litwack's *North of Slavery: The Negro in the Free States, 1790–1860* (Chicago and London: University of Chicago Press, 1961) and James and Lois Horton's *In Hope of Liberty: Culture, Community and Protest among Northern Free Blacks, 1700–1860* (New York: Oxford University Press, 1997) are excellent surveys of black life in the supposedly "free" North. On the South, Ira Berlin's *Slaves Without Masters: The Free Negro in the Antebellum South* (New York: Pantheon, 1974) is a model of careful scholarship. William Loren Katz's *The Black West: A Documentary and Pictorial History of the African American Role in the Expansion of the United States* (1971; reprint New York: Harlem Moon, 2005) is essential reading for anyone in search of a more inclusive account of life on the frontier.

Community studies give us insight into how black people struggled to win and then maintain their freedom at the local level. The following list is not meant to be exhaustive but simply to indicate how wide-ranging the scholarship is.

Baltimore: *Freedom's Port: The African American Community of Baltimore, 1790–1860* (Urbana and Chicago: University of Illinois Press, 1997).

Boston: James O. Horton and Lois E. Horton, *Black Bostonians: Family Life and Community Struggle in the Antebellum North* (2nd ed. New York: Holmes and Meier, 1999).

Florida: Jane Landers, *Black Society in Spanish Florida* (Urbana and Chicago: University of Illinois Press, 1999).

New Bedford: Kathryn Grover, *The Fugitive's Gibraltar: Escaping Slaves and Abolitionism in New Bedford, Massachusetts* (Amherst: University of Massachusetts Press, 2001).

New Orleans: Kimberly S. Hanger, *Bounded Lives, Bounded Places: Free Black Society in Colonial New Orleans, 1769–1803* (Durham: Duke University Press, 1997).

New York: Ira Berlin and Leslie M. Harris, eds., *Slavery in New York* (New York: The New Press, 2005).

Philadelphia: Gary B. Nash, *Forging Freedom: The Formation of Philadelphia's Black Community, 1720–1840* (Cambridge, Mass.: Harvard University Press, 1988).

St. Louis: Julie Winch, *The Clamorgans: One Family's History of Race in America* (New York: Hill & Wang, 2011).

For an excellent overview of free black life in the cities of the North, the South, and the Midwest, see Leonard P. Curry's *The Free Black in Urban America, 1800–1850: The Shadow of the Dream* (Chicago: University of Chicago Press, 1981).

Although the free black population was a heavily urbanized one by the mid-nineteenth century, most people of color lived in rural areas, as did the vast majority of whites. Melvin Patrick Ely's *Israel on the Appomattox: A Southern Experiment in Freedom* (New York: Vintage, 2005) is an intriguing study of one free black enclave and the unique set of circumstances that brought it into being. The experiences of black Midwestern farmers are chronicled in several books, the most accessible of which is Stephen A. Vincent's *Southern Seed, Northern Soil: African-American Farm Communities in the Midwest, 1765–1900* (Bloomington: Indiana University Press, 1999).

Black Americans were just as eager as whites to share in the American Dream of economic self-sufficiency. Loren Schweninger's *Black Property Owners in the South, 1790–1915* (Urbana and Chicago: University of Illinois Press, 1990) presents a fascinating picture of ingenuity and determination in the face of often overwhelming odds. W. Jeffrey Bolster's *Black Jacks: African American Seamen in the Age of Sail* (Cambridge, Mass.: Harvard University

Press, 1997) looks at the occupation that both challenged and sustained many African-American men and their families. Michael P. Johnson and James L. Roark recount the remarkable saga of the wealthy Ellison clan in *Black Masters: A Free Family of Color in the Old South* (New York: W. W. Norton, 1984), and in *Anna Madgigine Jai Kingsley: African Princess, Florida Slave, Plantation Owner* (Gainesville: University Press of Florida, 2010) Daniel L. Schafer tells the equally remarkable story of a slave who gained her freedom and became a rich planter with slaves of her own.

T. H. Breen and Stephen Innes's *"Myne Owne Ground": Race and Freedom on Virginia's Eastern Shore, 1640–1676* (New York: Oxford University Press, 1980) is a wonderfully nuanced account of the world the first black settlers to Virginia made for themselves during a time when enslavement for life was not a "given" for every black person. In *Black Yankees: The Development of an Afro-American Subculture in Eighteenth-Century New England* (Amherst: University of Massachusetts Press, 1988) William D. Piersen details the complexities of slavery and freedom in colonial New England, while Ira Berlin's prize-winning *Many Thousands Gone: the First Two Centuries of Slavery in North America* (Cambridge, Mass.: Harvard University Press, 1998) is a superb synthesis that explains not only how different slave systems evolved in colonial America but how some black people managed to locate the weak spots in those systems and extricate themselves from bondage.

On the struggle for independence and the role of African Americans in that struggle, the classic study is Benjamin Quarles's *The Negro in the American Revolution* (Chapel Hill: University of North Carolina Press, 1961). Black involvement in the Revolution has continued to intrigue historians, and all of the following books are highly recommended: Edward Countryman, *Enjoy the Same Liberty: Black Americans and the Revolutionary Era* (Lanham, Md: Rowman and Littlefield, 2012); J. William Harris, *The Hanging of Thomas Jeremiah: A Free Black Man's Encounter with Liberty* (New Haven: Yale University Press, 2009); Woody Holton, *Black Americans in the Revolutionary Era* (Boston and New York: Bedford/St. Martin's, 2009), Sidney Kaplan and Emma Nogrady Kaplan, *The Black Presence in the Era of the American Revolution* (Amherst: University of Massachusetts Press, 1989), and Simon Schama, *Rough Crossings: The Slaves, the British, and the American Revolution* (New York: Harper, 2007).

On black activism to end slavery and discrimination, see Benjamin Quarles's *Black Abolitionists* (New York: Oxford University Press, 1969) and a more recent work, Patrick Rael's *Black Identity and Black Protest in the Antebellum North* (Chapel Hill: University of North Carolina Press,

2002), as well as individual biographies, of which the following are just a sampling:

Richard Allen: Richard S. Newman, *Freedom's Prophet: Bishop Richard Allen, the AME Church, and the Black Founding Fathers* (New York: New York University Press, 2008).

Mary Ann Shadd Cary: Jane Rhodes, *Mary Ann Shadd Cary: The Black Press and Protest in the Nineteenth Century* (Bloomington: Indiana University Press, 1999).

Paul Cuffe: Lamont D. Thomas, *Rise to Be a People: A Biography of Paul Cuffe* (Urbana and Chicago: University of Illinois Press, 1986).

James Forten: Julie Winch, *A Gentleman of Color: The Life of James Forten* (New York: Oxford University Press, 2002).

John Brown Russwurm: Winston James, *The Struggles of John Brown Russwurm: The Life and Writings of a Pan-Africanist Pioneer, 1799–1851* (New York: New York University Press, 2010).

Maria W. Stewart: Marilyn Richardson, *Maria W. Stewart: America's First Black Woman Political Writer: Essays and Speeches* (Bloomington: Indiana University Press, 1987).

David Walker: Peter P. Hinks, *To Awaken My Afflicted Brethren: David Walker and the Problem of Antebellum Slave Resistance* (University Park: Pennsylvania State University Press, 1997).

Many of the same forces that shaped the lives of free black men shaped the lives of free black women, but their gender meant that they had to contend with the "double bond" of being black and female in a society that privileged whiteness and masculinity. In addition to the biographies of individual women listed above, readers should look at Susan Lebsock's *The Free Women of Petersburg: Status and Culture in a Southern Town, 1784–1860* (New York: W. W. Norton, 1984) and Wilma King's *The Essence of Liberty: Free Black Women During the Slave Era* (Columbia: University of Missouri Press, 2006).

The best sources for trying to understand how free people of color saw their situation in America are obviously their own writings. Two semi-autobiographical novels that give us glimpses into the lives of two very different people are Frank J. Webb's *The Garies and Their Friends* (1857) and Harriet E. Wilson's *Our Nig; or, Sketches from the Life of a Free Black* (1859). Both are available in modern paperback editions. A number of women and men left journals and memoirs. See, for example, Brenda Stevenson, ed., *The Journals of Charlotte Forten Grimké* (New York: Oxford University Press, 1988), William R. Hogan and Edwin Adams Davis, eds.,

William Johnson's Natchez: The Antebellum Diary of a Free Negro (Baton Rouge: Louisiana State University Press, 1993), and Loren Schweninger, ed., *From Tennessee Slave to St. Louis Entrepreneur: The Autobiography of James Thomas* (Columbia: University of Missouri Press, 1984). Dorothy B. Porter's *Early Negro Writing, 1760–1837* (1971; reprint Baltimore: Black Classic Press, 1995) gathers together dozens of otherwise hard-to-find pamphlets and speeches by free women and men of color. In *Pamphlets of Protest: An Anthology of Early African American Protest Literature, 1790–1860* (New York and London: Routledge, 2001), Richard S. Newman, Patrick Rael, and Phillip Lapsansky have expanded upon Porter's work. Two very useful online databases that contain hundreds of documents by and about free black people are the Early American Imprints series, available as part of the Archive of Americana collection at www.readex.com and Documenting the American South at http://docsouth.unc.edu. The sheer size of the document database gathered by C. Peter Ripley and his team at the Black Abolitionist Papers Project should not deter anyone from exploring it. One of the guiding principles of the Project has always been *access*. The entire BAP Archive is searchable for free through http://research.udmercy.edu. African-American and abolitionist newspapers reveal what truly mattered to free people of color in the antebellum era. Accessible Archives (www.accessible.com) contains transcriptions of a number of important newspapers, including *Freedom's Journal*, the *Colored American*, and Frederick Douglass's *North Star*. Two collections of convention minutes, Howard H. Bell, ed., *Minutes of the Proceedings of the National Negro Conventions, 1830–1864* (New York: Arno Press, 1969), and the two-volume *Proceedings of the Black State Conventions, 1840–1865* (Philadelphia: Temple University Press, 1979 and 1985), edited by Philip S. Foner and George E. Walker, reflect the issues and concerns of African Americans at the national and local levels. On the outcry over the agenda of the American Colonization Society see the speeches and petitions in William Lloyd Garrison's *Thoughts on African Colonization*. Originally published in 1832, it is available through http://books.google.com. Given the rapid pace at which primary materials are being put online, anyone interested in delving more deeply into different aspects of free black life should have no shortage of resources, most of them just a mouse click away.

~

Index

~

About the Author

Julie Winch is professor of history at the University of Massachusetts Boston, where she has taught since 1985. She has published five books on the lives of free people of African descent in eighteenth- and nineteenth-century America, including *The Clamorgans: One Family's History of Race in America* and *A Gentleman of Color: The Life of James Forten.* She has been the recipient of fellowships from the National Endowment for the Humanities, the American Antiquarian Society, the John Carter Brown Library, Mystic Seaport, and the Beinecke Library. Her biography of James Forten won the American Historical Association's Wesley-Logan Prize.